Dr. Marcella Bakur Weiner is a psychotherapist and an adjunct professor at the City University of New York. She has worked extensively as a clinician with the elderly and their families, as a senior research scientist for the New York State Department of Mental Hygiene, and with geriatric patients in hospitals and nursing homes. She has taught on the psychology of aging at Columbia University and has trained and lectured to large audiences in the United States and abroad. She is the author of *Working with the Aged* (Prentice-Hall) and co-author of *The Starr-Weiner Report on Sex and Sexuality in the Mature Years.*

Dr. Jeanne Teresi has training and experience in clinical gerontology and in measurement and statistics. Her current primary involvement is in research. She is a senior research scientist for Columbia University Center for Geriatrics and Gerontology at New York State Psychiatric Institute, and senior researcher for the consulting firm Community Research Applications.

Corrine Streich is an award-winning international author/journalist who has written extensively on current social issues as well as on art and auctions, food, and travel.

Prentice-Hall International, Inc., *London*
Prentice-Hall of Australia Pty. Limited, *Sydney*
Prentice-Hall Canada Inc., *Toronto*
Prentice-Hall of India Private Limited, *New Delhi*
Prentice-Hall of Japan, Inc., *Tokyo*
Prentice-Hall of Southeast Asia Pte. Ltd., *Singapore*
Whitehall Books Limited, *Wellington, New Zealand*
Editora Prentice-Hall do Brasil Ltda., *Rio de Janeiro*

Marcella Bakur Weiner
Jeanne Teresi
with Corrine Streich

Old People Are a Burden, But Not My Parents

A SPECTRUM BOOK

Prentice-Hall, Inc., Englewood Cliffs, New Jersey 07632

Library of Congress Cataloging in Publication Data
Bakur Weiner, Marcella.
  Old people are a burden, but not my parents.

  "A Spectrum Book."
  Includes index.
  1. Aged—United States.   2. Aged—Mental health.
3. Aged—Psychology.   4. Aged—Family relationships.
I. Teresi, Jeanne.   II. Streich, Corinne.   III. Title.
HQ1064.U5B23   1983   305.2'6   82-23034
ISBN 0-13-633818-6
ISBN 0-13-633800-3 (pbk.)

© 1983 by Prentice-Hall, Inc., Englewood Cliffs, New Jersey 07632.
All rights reserved. No part of this book may be reproduced in any form
or by any means without permission in writing from the publisher.
A Spectrum Book. Printed in the United States of America.

10 9 8 7 6 5 4 3 2 1

ISBN 0-13-633800-3

ISBN 0-13-633818-6 {PBK.}

Chapter One: "When I'm Sixty-Four" (John Lennon and Paul McCartney)
© 1967 Northern Songs Limited. All rights for the U.S.A., Mexico, and the
Philippines controlled by Maclean Music, Inc., c/o ATV Music Corp. Used
by permission. All rights reserved.
Chapter Three: "A Song in Time of Depression" (From the Paiute).
Permissions secured in 1918 by Boni & Liveright, Inc. for "The Path on
the Rainbow."
Chapter Six: Ashley Montague, *Growing Young*. New York: McGraw-Hill
Book Company, 1981, p. 199. Reprinted by permission.
Chapter Seven: "The Quarrel" by Stanely Kunitz. From *The Poems of
Stanley Kunitz*, 1928-78. © 1978 by Stanley Kunitz. First appeared
in *The Atlantic*, reprinted by permission of Little, Brown and Company
in association with The Atlantic Monthly Press.

Editorial production supervision: Marlys Lehmann
Cover design: © 1983 by Jeannette Jacobs
Manufacturing buyer: Cathie Lenard

This book is available at a special discount when ordered in
bulk quantities. Contact Prentice-Hall, Inc., General
Publishing Division, Special Sales, Englewood Cliffs, N.J. 07632.

To my sister, Dorothy, and brother (in-law), Jack Kessler, who were loving models for me in my own aging at every stage of life.

Marcella Bakur Weiner

To my parents for their continuing support and encouragement.

Jeanne Teresi

To Frank, Nina, and Lori.

Corrine Streich

Contents

Preface/*xi*

Chapter One   AGING IN OUR TIME/*1*
Longevity: A Stunning Achievement/2   Aging and Family Life-Style/3   Normal Aging: How Many Older People Are Dependent?/4   The Family Role as Care-Giver/5   Growing Old in a Changing Society/6   Individual Basic Needs and Emotional Responses/7   The Future Family Network/8

Chapter Two   THE FAMILY EGO AND ADAPTATION TO CHANGE/*11*
Parents as Regulators of Feelings and Behavior/12   A Divided Family Ego/14   The Controlling Son/15   The Overly Dutiful Daughter/16   Trying to Reverse the Past/19   The Dependent Wife/20   Aging and Self-Image/22   An Awareness of Pain/23

Chapter Three   SENILE DEMENTIA/*25*
The Stages of Dementia/27   Classic Core Symptoms/29   Types of Dementia/29   Causes of Dementia/31   Incidence Rates/32   Individual Reactions to the Onset of Dementia/33

Variables in Behavior/34 Clinical Assessment of Functional Capacity/38 Psychiatric Diagnostic Techniques/41 Medical Diagnostic Techniques/42 Mistaken Diagnoses/43 Treatment/46

Chapter Four **BEHAVIORAL PROBLEMS/49**
Emotional Disturbances/51 Affective Disorders/52 Somatic Disorders/59 Cognitive Disorders/59 Paranoid Disorders/60 Psychoses and Primitive Impulses/62 Assessing the Risks of Disturbed Behavior/64

Chapter Five **RELATING TO THE DISTURBED OLDER PERSON/67**
Listening Beyond What They Are Saying/69 One-Sided Conversations/70 Understanding Your Own Feelings/71 A Scenario/72 Reality Orientation as a Helpful Approach/74 Love and Hate Can Go Together/75

Chapter Six **NURSING HOME PLACEMENT AND FAMILY DECISIONS/77**
Family Roles in Decision Making/78 Cooperation and Compromise: A Case Example/79 The Burden of Guilt/81 Including the Older Person in Decision Making/82 Looking for a Suitable Facility/83 Institutional Levels of Care/83 The Nursing Home Population/85 Staff-Patient Relationships/87 The Transition from Home to Nursing Home/88 The Family as a Link Between Patient and Staff/89 Coping Strategies for Patient and Family/90 Complaining Is a Form of Communicating/91 Visiting Your Relative/92 Relocation Can Be Stressful/93 New Responses to Old Problems/94

Chapter Seven	**CRITICAL PERIODS IN THE FAMILY**/97	

When Family Roles Change/98   Longtime Conflicts: Mother-Daughter Interaction/99   The "Life Review"/102   Looking Beyond Behavior/103   The Masks of Aging: Equating Old Age with Illness/104   The Chronic Complainer/105   Symptoms of Needs/105   Age Is Not a Deterrent to Treatment/107

Chapter Eight	**RETIREMENT**/109	

Retirement as a New Phenomenon/110   Health and Well-Being/111   Self-Esteem: Losses and Gains/112   Research Findings on Retirement/114   Mental Adjustments: A Case Study/116   The Right to Work/117

Chapter Nine	**MOURNING AND AFTERWARD**/119	

Family Stages/120   The Fear of Separation/121   Predictable Patterns/122   Surviving a Death in the Family/122   Helping the Widowed/123   Loss of a Parent/124   Adaptation to Living Alone/124   Resourceful Living/125   Sexuality in the Later Years/128   Limitations to Sexuality for the Older Woman/129

Chapter Ten	**THE YOUNG/OLD**/131	

The Elderly Are a Diverse Group/132   Aging Does Not Mean Disengagement/134   What Do You Expect at Your Age?/135   History Influences the Way We Are/136   Personality and Life Events/138   The New Breed of Older People/138

Chapter Eleven	**THE FRAIL ELDERLY**/143	

Becoming Dependent/144   Coping with Emergencies/146   Alternative Living

Arrangements/147 The Family as Primary Care-Giver/147 Dealing with Bureaucracy/148 How Long Can Families Continue to Cope?/150 The Institution and the Person/151 What Ever Happened to the Concept of Wisdom in Old Age?/153 Medical Attitudes Toward the Elderly/154

Chapter Twelve THE MYTHOLOGY OF AGING/157
Perceptions of Old Age/158 Do We Really Care?/161 More Ambivalences/162 Historical Views/163 Always Looking for the Fountain of Youth/166 Fact and Fiction/167 Television and Ageism/168 Age Discrimination in the Work Place/169 Age Stereotyping and Personnel Decisions/170 Societal Attitudes and Social Security/171

APPENDIX/175
A Statistical Overview of the Older Population and Family Support Systems/175

References/*181*

Index/*187*

Preface

Our primary purpose in writing this book is to provide insights and guidelines for everyone concerned with the well-being of an older person, whether that person lives alone, within the family, or in a protective-care setting. We offer a comprehensive picture of old age in our society today that is designed to help family members gain a clear idea of the behavioral changes and problems inherent in growing old. The experiences of other people have always been a most effective learning tool, and we use case histories in order to define some of the most prevalent problems. Of course, these case histories do not always have happy endings, but even in the most extreme examples, we explore approaches to meeting the dependency needs of older individuals while considering the well-being of the entire family. Each generation has distinct characteristics that make it interesting and different and that contribute to the development of the next generation.

We also examine research showing contradictions between society's attitudes toward older people in general and the behavior of individuals toward older family members. Evidence for this research gave us the title of our book, *Old People Are a Burden, But Not My Parents*. It is apparent that Americans are deeply concerned about their elderly kin and are their main care-givers. Therefore, it is important that they recognize the differences between normal aging and problem aging, distinctions we make throughout our book. For instance, in the chapter on senile dementia, we define this disease, its prevalence, the characteristics of its onset and development; and we distinguish between true dementias and those symptoms of pseudodementias that have different causes and often can be treated with some success.

Communicating with a mentally impaired older person can be extremely difficult and trying, and we have written simple dialogues to facilitate conversation and interaction. Throughout, we try to present an understanding of the dynamics of growth and aging in terms of the individual, the family, and society. We have addressed our book to a wide audience. It aims to meet the needs of the general reader who may feel helpless and alone while caring for an aged person, and to provide information for those who want to know what to anticipate and how to plan for their own old age.

We have also provided research data and survey reports for further study by students of gerontology, regardless of academic disciplines. The book should be of use to health professionals (nurses, social workers, and other practicing clinicians) as well as to researchers, because we provide both practical information about how to clinically treat the older person and statistical resource information for those involved in research.

Our book has a dual focus; to provide practical suggestions for coping with the dependency problems of the frail elderly and at the same time to present a profile of the healthy and independent mature adult against a background of social change in our society today. Our hope is that this interpretation will help to lessen some of the fears of growing old, while recognizing that older people are a diverse group whose changing needs are inevitable.

Acknowledgments

We each owe a great deal to the many people who contributed to this book, and together we give special thanks to our editor,

John Hunger, whose creative ideas and constructive criticism helped to shape our original concept into a book. In particular, we want to thank Clare Juddson Kagel for her advice and helpful comments (MBW); Peter Cross, for reading and critiquing several sections of the manuscript (JT); and Adele and Howard Goodkind and Rosemary Okun for their insights and encouragement (CS). We also thank our typists, Harriet Ayers and Susan Friedman, for their patience and cheerful availability.

*Look to the past for only then
     can your work serve as a model for the future.
Let us seek the past,
Be an age
That cherishes the old
Then our "today," one day
Will be someone's "long ago."*

Saigyo Hōshi (Twelfth Century)
from *Sixty-Four Tanka*

Chapter One

Aging in Our Time

*When I get older losing my hair,
Many years from now,
Will you still be sending me a Valentine
Birthday greetings bottle of wine . . .
Will you still need me—will you still feed me
When I'm sixty-four.*

Lennon and McCartney

The aging of America is a phenomenon to which many of us respond with mixed feelings of hopefulness, pride, and apprehension. Although medical science has been successful in dramatically extending the average life span, comparatively little has been done to insure that people live out the later years of their lives productively, securely, and with the maximum enjoyment. Now that we can prolong life, we are beginning to worry about the aging of America, when the traditional population pyramid is turned upside down and the old begin to outnumber the young. While struggling to keep the elderly alive as long as possible, the price of longevity for many has been a decline in the quality of their lives because of isolation, financial distress, and chronic illness, arising in part from complex and often contradictory attitudes toward aging and the aged. These attitudes are derived from myriad factors such as individual, subconscious motivations; social learning; economics; the media; and above all, from the old people we have known and our relationships with them.

Longevity: A Stunning Achievement

Human beings have always had the potential to live about ninety years, more or less, but only in recent years have large numbers begun to fulfill this potential. Studies show that a child born in the United States in 1900 could expect to live forty-seven years. Today the average age is seventy-three years. The stunning increase of twenty-six years in life expectancy in this century is the result of disease control, of reducing the risks of dying during childbirth and infancy through improved environmental sanitation, and of improved nutrition. Epidemics of bacterial pneumonia, smallpox, diphtheria, and cholera no longer decimate the population, thanks to prevention, not cure. Among the leading causes of disability and death today are heart disease, cancer, stroke, hypertension, and diabetes. Some of these current health problems are brought on by social pressures and environmental factors, by obesity, alcohol and drug abuse, and other factors which safety regulations and a more disciplined life-style may be able to better control. Although there is no guarantee that changing life habits for the sake of health will keep people hale and hearty for seventy-three years or longer, the odds are better for those who reduce the risks most strongly associated with disability and premature death.

Aging and Family Life-Style

The manner or style in which we cope with various aspects of aging is consistent with the ways in which we live within our families. If members have been secretive and competitive; if they have been frightened to show their emotions, or have lived in the shadow of domineering parents; if they were unable to be supportive of one another, then dependency of an older relative could cause problems for the entire family.
    A son, for example, who had a strong dependency relationship with his mother as a child, may be consumed with guilt about placing her in a nursing home although she is clearly in need of it. A man who is fearful of death may use denial as a defense, refusing to recognize that his mother is seriously ill and in need of completing a life-review process before death, thus denying her the final chance to express her feelings about dying and of attaining some closure in their relationship.

Some people accept the responsibility of nurturing their sick elderly relatives with patience and affection, whereas others are unable to cope with the demanding day-to-day care of the frail elderly but will find a suitable long-term-care facility for them. Contrary to one of the most prevalent myths about aging, few families neglect their elderly kin. They do, of course, bring to their relationships with them their own concepts of what old age means and their own defenses in dealing with fears they have about growing old themselves. For many elderly people, a major fear is loss of control over their lives. This worry can be particularly acute for those with limited mobility who need another person to help them with personal care activities, or activities of daily living (ADL), the term used by health professionals.

These fears are common, yet few people seriously plan ahead for the exigencies of the later years until faced with a sudden accident or illness. The situation becomes an emergency, and often they do not have enough time to consider the best solutions. When the crisis is resolved, they may not want to look back and review their actions and the alternatives. Instead, they ignore the possibilities until once again faced with the urgency of a similar situation. In the everyday lives of many people, old age is simply not relevant or interesting, and many admit to finding the subject so depressing that they would rather not think about it at all.

Moreover, these feelings are reinforced by society's attitudes. Until very recently, old people were virtually invisible. In a society such as ours, which places great importance on youth and vigor, on economic productiveness, on sexual and social competitiveness, old age is viewed as undesirable, as a time of lessening attractiveness, health, and social worth.

Normal Aging: How Many Older People Are Dependent?

If we were to ask ourselves and our friends to estimate the proportion of people over the age of sixty-five who are senile and unable to care for themselves, the number would be predictably high, based on responses collected in national public opinion polls over many years. The actual figure is quite low. For example, only 5 percent of the older population (over sixty-five years) are, at any time, confined in nursing homes. (This percentage does increase with age, and about 23 percent of individuals over age 65 will spend some time in a nursing home during their lifetime.) Moreover, the majority of community-resident older adults (92 to 95 percent of the noninstitutionalized) manage on their own, or with only a little assistance. Why we continue to believe otherwise may relate to our mythology of aging, or ageism as it is sometimes called, a phenomenon we will explore in later chapters.

It is difficult to get a true picture of "normal" aging because either we are made aware of the problems of only the frail and the helpless, or we are shown geriatric *wunderkinder*—octogenerian balloonists, round-the-world sailors, and the like. And always, older people are considered within the framework of our value system, which venerates youth and places more emphasis and energy into staying cosmetically young. Rather than admiring what age adds to faces, we fret about what it takes away. Perhaps someday medical science will be able to keep each of us in the peak of health, vigor, and sexuality until the day our biological clock is switched off, and then we will quickly, painlessly, and neatly disintegrate. Until medical science catches up with science fiction, we shall have to look for solutions to the day-to-day physical and emotional aspects of growing old in our changing society.

The Family Role as Care-Giver

Families have traditionally been the primary care-givers of the elderly, but in recent years the government has also helped by creating social welfare services to dispense aid to the elderly who are in various stages of need. These services, instead of usurping family responsibilities, have actually created a new role for kin as mediators between the institutional bureaucracies and their elderly relatives. Without this family help, many older people would not be able to deal with the intricacies of the service agency structures, nor would a surprisingly large number of the elderly be willing to accept the help that is forthcoming. Raised in the early part of this century, before the development of social welfare services, they do not believe that they are legitimately entitled to the funds that are offered, and many of the elderly view these funds as charity or handouts which their pride will not allow them to take. Often they would not accept what is due to them but for the intervention of their younger kin.

As the network of government and private social service agencies has grown, the proportion of younger family caregivers has declined through decreases in the birth rate and increases in longevity, and because the traditional helper of olden days, the "dutiful daughter," now often takes an active role in the work force and is not as available in the home as before. Despite these social changes, the emotional ties of affection and the need for parental approval at any age continue to dominate our lives.

No one has dictated that children must provide care for their elders, yet for the most part this care is forthcoming and handed down in the tradition and values of a particular family system. Emotional ties are made early and remain fairly constant; ultimately, it is these emotional ties that create and sustain family cohesion, whether those connections were made biologically or by choice.

Growing Old in a Changing Society

We are living through a time of great change, allowing many choices in life-style. Diversity and eclecticism exist in every form of social and governmental structure. One can still uphold the traditional pattern of the extended American family—a mother and a father with two children and grandparents living nearby. But divorce and separation are no longer uncommon, and we also see smaller households and two-paycheck families; unmarried couples living together; divorced or single men and women heading their own households; husbands wanting and getting custody of their children. Today people are having and will have more complicated relationships; they are learning to tolerate life-styles very different from their own.

Already we can see an increasing mobility not just among the younger generations, but among the middle-aged and the "young old" as well. Often, today, the grandmother as well as the grandfather are still working through their late sixties at jobs away from home; and when they retire, they do not stay near their children but may move to leisure villages in warm climates. Researchers from a variety of disciplines are measuring, calculating, and assessing what impact these changes and multiple relationships will have on American society.

As the rate of change has accelerated, time more than distance has created differences among people. For example, anthropologists have noted that tribal groups developed entirely different mythologies, rituals, and symbols, although they lived in close proximity to one another. Yet within each tribe, there was virtually no variation in rituals, symbols and values over long periods of time and over many generations. We are witnessing quite a different phenomenon today, in that both space and time seem to be contracting. Jean-clad students from backgrounds as different and as geographically distant as Brooklyn and Botswana have more in common with one another than they do with their own grandparents and sometimes even with their own parents.

Consider a multigenerational family in a typical large American city: The grandparents emigrated from a small town in a distant country with nothing but the hope of finding work in "the land of opportunity." Religion and family ties were the core of their existence. In old age, many of them remained poor and uneducated. If they lived on their own, they probably would not be able to make their way through the present intricacies of the hierarchical social service structures, nor would they try, for as we mentioned, they do not understand that they are entitled to welfare services. Their middle-aged son is also a family man who believes that it is his responsibility to take care of his parents, but he expects some government support for them. His goals and expectations for himself are much higher than those of his parents. He has still higher expectations for his son: Giving him a good education is one of his priorities. As he grows up, this young man and his grandparents have very little in common except love and affection. They do not share the same native language and may not have the same social attitudes or religious beliefs. The young man expects to achieve status and financial success. His grandparents have been poor and are grateful for what they have.

Individual Basic Needs and Emotional Responses

Nevertheless, the young and the old have the same basic needs for love and affection even though they experienced them in different environments and with changing perceptions. Most people born in the early part of this century were raised to believe in the inviolability of marriage. Although no longer entirely disapproving of the divorces of others, including their own children's or grandchildren's, they themselves may not be able to understand the principles of individual determination and mutual consent that make divorce increasingly possible in our society. Rather than divorce, they may have lived for years in a state of total estrangement. Sometimes, however, a crisis occurs, perhaps the mortal illness of one of them, and this becomes an occasion for reexamining and reaffirming their lives together. The reverse can also happen. Two older adults may enjoy intimacy and a generally reciprocal relationship whereby each exerts sufficient power and mastery to continue the family in its desired patterns and goals. The onset of a severe illness can destroy this mutuality by putting one of them in a position of only receiving care, while the other is forced always to be the care-giver. Where lack of flexibility is a family pattern, conflict may arise.

The children may be called upon for help. They are themselves middle-aged and becoming aware of incipient pressures and physical decrements in their own lives. But if they have been in the habit of helping their parents, they may see their primary role as care-givers. Their children also may feel compelled to cater to their grandparents' needs.

Many people are unable to love the old, even when the old people are their own parents. They may take responsibility for them and show concern, but at the same time they can suffer a kind of emotional shock and resentment at what they feel to be a reversal of roles. They may feel imprisoned by the endless need to care for those who, through illness and incapacity, are freed from all duty to them. Even if a parent enters a nursing home, the middle-aged child can still suffer from a strange sense of imprisonment and seldom visit or not visit at all. Sometimes they have already experienced a mourning process for the incurably ill parent, and they do not want to become reinvolved. This can result in feelings of unresolved, partial grief; family members should be helped to realize that it is all right to feel this way, and that by talking, they may discover what concrete tasks they can perform so that they can get in touch with their feelings for their parents once again.

The Future Family Network

As people have fewer children and live longer, there will be many families with only one adult child to care for two parents, or adults with no children and no spouse or siblings to turn to. If changing family styles continue to influence our ability or need to enter into multiple relationships, a wider network of support for the elderly will be found through more distant kinships and through friendships.

With life-styles in flux, family systems and individuals undergo continual changes and pressures to either "stay the same" or to "change with the times." In view of the concentration on the quality of life's experiences and on our ability to prolong life, we are now faced with the responsibility for decisions on issues for which a short while ago we had no choice.

Life can be extended with the use of increasingly sophisticated medical techniques. Deaths are more protracted now. The old were not the only ones who were vulnerable to death when childbirth and infant mortality rates were high. But today, death occurs mainly among the old and from chronic and lingering diseases such as cancer and heart ailments. Patients are usually no longer kept at home, but are treated in hospitals where they can see their families only at appointed visiting hours. Even when the odds for recovery are low, families are not always given the choice of whether or not to pursue an action that might result in shortening the life of a terminally ill patient. The trauma is great to relatives watching a loved one being kept alive, only to deteriorate beyond recognition. Yet often they feel helpless when confronted with the attitude of many doctors, including those practicing geriatric medicine, that death is a manifestation of the failure of medicine.

With the development of attitudes that provide a new synthesis of the best way to care for the dying, families are beginning to have some choice between doctors who feel that no matter how complicated, uncomfortable, and of dubious values the efforts are, it is their duty to save and preserve life, and doctors who feel it is their duty to treat death and dying with the same respect as life and living.

In the chapters that follow, we will explore the aging process through the concept of generation and family life. In drawing upon case histories and statistical evidence, we will attempt to present as complete a picture as possible without resorting to a scant "either-or" solution to the highly emotional and controversial aspects of aging and family life. Our premise is that although there is no one model for a successfully functioning family, the *family*, whether it is connected through biology or by choice, is still the most intense force from which we get meaning in our lives.

Chapter Two

The Family Ego and Adaptation to Change

One of the major findings of social research in aging in all western countries has been the rediscovery of the important role of the family in old age....
Ethel Shanas (1979)

The family, in simplest terms, consists of two or more people united by ties of marriage and parenthood. The most basic unit (sometimes referred to as a nuclear or conjugal unit) is comprised of a woman, a man, and their children. The family is also society's most complex organizational structure, as well as the most important source of emotional security and interdependence. Each man and woman brings from his and her parental home a set of ideals and expectations of which they may not be totally aware, yet these ideals strongly influence the atmosphere of the home they make together and their attitudes toward their children. No family, as no individual, is free from problems, but each family has its own way of solving them, and this depends largely on the quality of the relationship between the man and the woman.

Parents as Regulators
of Feelings and Behavior

The parents' role is to educate and socialize their children, to regulate their behavior, and to impart to them the values and symbols that are crucial to their culture. Parents are responsible for insuring that their children conform to and share certain basic values so family members can relate to one another in an open way, free from ambiguity. In such an atmosphere, emotional attachments develop and the home is a sanctuary protected from the pressures of the outside world, where parents and children make one another feel good, relaxed, and accepted. Positive feelings toward the world in general, toward achievement and cooperation, as well as positive feelings toward older people and old age may be engendered in such an atmosphere.

The family is the core of existence to a young child. If its parents are unreliable and inconsistent in their timing, their reactions, and their behaviors, then the child may feel the world in general is unloving, uncaring, and not to be trusted. Throughout life, this child may look for and deliberately uncover evidence to prove this view of life, and generations later, as a parent and then as a grandparent, continue to impart a negative and rigid system of behavior to its own family of origin. Clinical anecdotes abound with such examples: A man, speaking of his third marriage, says that his wife, too, is "just like the others—ungiving, unloving, and untrustworthy." Psychotherapy may make him aware that he did the choosing of each marriage partner and that he now is imitating or reenacting an old scene in an attempt to master it and to feel some control over his live.

Within the boundaries engendered by home and family are certain enduring psychological structures which, for purposes of illustration, can be compared within the Freudian interpretation of the individual psyche. Freud separated the psyche into three hypothetical structures: the *ego*, the *id*, and the *superego*. The *ego* (representing external reality) receives information, processes it, integrates it, and then acts as logical mediator between the demands of the *id* (the pleasure-seeking mass of blind instincts and contradictory impulses in the unconscious) and the demands of the *superego* (which acts as a conscience in terms of societal values, morals, customs, and ideals). Just as each individual develops his or her own perceptions of the inner and outer worlds and how to integrate them, so too does the family develop a collective way of mediating between its inner and outer realities. The family ego, or the collective ego, does not develop in isolation but comes from the shared perceptions, ties, bonds, and linkages of one generation to the next. Thus, each individual is endowed not only with an inherent genetic structure, but also with an enduring, often unconscious, family way of thinking, feeling, and experiencing.

In a caring family, the collective ego, grown out of the natural consolidation of the strength of its members, unites common experiences and capabilities for the good of all. This family, with its strong coping skills, can accept the natural progression of life's changes. While life is by no means problem-free, it may seem so to outsiders because of the evident supportiveness and solidarity of its members.

A Divided Family Ego

While some families may be divided, with members quarreling and fighting, other families may have such strong ties among members that they isolate themselves and withdraw from the larger world around them. In order to maintain tight control of its life and to cope with changes and events in the outside world, this frightened family established rigid attitudes and patterns of behavior to which all members must adhere. For example, they may believe that the world is a treacherous place, not to be trusted, and allow only negative criteria into their lives for observation, consideration, and action. Any evidence to the contrary may be briefly examined but quickly discarded. Contradictions are not tolerated, as they threaten the basic core of existence. Family members cling to each other in their need for protection and as a buffer against the outside world.

The following examples from case histories are used to illustrate how family patterns of behavior influence perceptions of dependency and adaptation to one's own aging.

The Controlling Son

A fifty-eight-year-old son, seeking counsel for his frail, elderly mother, continually made changes even after suitable arrangements had been organized for the woman's comfort. His mother stayed in her own home, in the care of a nurse's aide, under the supervision of the family doctor. She seemed generally content, but cried whenever her son was ready to leave after his weekly visit.

The son interpreted this crying, and her sporadic forgetfulness and occasional incontinence, as desperate signs that needed to be remedied. Each time he visited, he tried to make some change in his mother's schedule or diet to try to alleviate what he saw as "most distressing symptoms."

He told a family therapist, "My mother is failing. She is not what she used to be. I see changes and it worries me." The therapist pointed out that since his mother was ninety-two years old, changes were inevitable. It was then suggested that he seek short-term therapy for himself.

This tense, impatient man, twice married and twice divorced, grew up in what seemed to him to be an action-oriented family. His father, a high school athletic coach, saw to it that every minute of his young son's day was accounted for. When he did not behave in accordance with his father's harsh rules, the boy was severely punished. He remembered being sent home from school ill, yet carrying out his daily chores because not doing so would have resulted in pain and humiliation.

Though his father died suddenly of a heart attack when he was in his middle years, and his only sibling, an older sister, was also dead, the son continued to react to situations in ways that were both familiar and familial. He had no tolerance for change, for mistakes, for waiting, for anything less than "taking immediate action and handling the situation." He often used this phrase during therapy sessions and repeatedly said, "I keep telling her not to do that. She should know better by now," when he referred to his mother's changeability of mood and incontinence. His own frustration and anger at her, for being ninety-two years old and for having shortcomings, infuriated and frightened him. He asked if he would end up that way when he was old, stating that he drank "too much" and took tranquilizers when anxiety pushed at him.

The son's conflicts were explored in terms of his family history, of their unrelenting need for total control, and of his mother's symptoms appearing to him as willful lack of control. Heir to his father's will or ego, he was impelled to make irrational demands of himself and his mother in a reenactment of scenes from childhood. In this action-oriented family, "doing nothing" or waiting provoked anxiety. Action represented strength, and anything short of that was a sign of weakness.

Therapy gave him the time to pause and think about what he was feeling, at last to give himself the time he deserved. He became, in time, more accepting and tolerant of himself and also less impatient with his mother. He left therapy soon after his mother's death. Whether or not these new insights were of a lasting nature is difficult to determine, yet some progress was noted despite an original maladaptive family system.

The maladaptive (or unhealthy) family ego may develop in an environment in which communication is sadly lacking. In a healthy family, communication is open and a set of rules known to all. The consequences for breaking these rules are understood, allowing individual members to make their own decisions where possible. Not threatened by fears of separation from the group if they disagree with one another, individuals are, on the whole, considerate and cooperative.

The Overly Dutiful Daughter

Conversely, when communication is lacking, family members operate as a group of disparate individuals who pretend to live by the rules. But since these rules are never understood, shared, or openly expressed, individuals hide their feelings and adhere to their own secret agenda. Sally Green* was part of such a family. Her parents clung together in what seemed to be a negative bond of mutual disagreements and needs, each competing in the role of authority while contradicting each other, neither taking responsibility for the joint well-being of the other or for their children.

As a child, Sally's parents worked long hours in a neighborhood store that they owned. Consequently, there were no set hours for meals; her mother never went to school on the day parents were invited; birthdays were usually forgotten. Sally, fastidious by nature, tried from the time she could wield a mop and bucket to clean and tidy up the household dirt and disorder her parents seemed to take for granted. "You can eat off the floor in my store," her mother was proud to state. It was true, Sally admitted, but you could not eat off the dining table at home unlesss she, Sally, cleaned it first.

Often, the moment her parents came from work, they began to quarrel over the day's events, and Sally's father, a weak man with a volatile temper, would harangue his wife for not having dinner ready and for being a terrible housekeeper. In his anger, he would throw things around, adding to the existing chaos. Her mother would scream, "If you were a real man, I wouldn't have to go out to work all day!" During these bitter fights, Sally and her younger sister cowered in their bedroom, miserable, hungry, waiting in fear and unexpressed anger. Sally described all this during sessions with a therapist whose help she had sought soon after placing her mother in a nursing home. The real problem, Sally maintained, was that her mother was not adjusting to life in the facility. However, instead of considering ways to alleviate this problem, Sally's solution was to take her out of the facility and get her back to her own apartment as soon as possible, against medical advice.

The mother had been placed in the nursing home after an illness and after abusing many live-in homemakers with insults and attempts at physical assault. She also suffered from fre-

*All names in case histories have been changed.

quent bouts of incontinence. Since placement, Sally spent a few hours every day visiting her mother.

She had not told the therapist about these constant visits because, she explained, she thought it would be obvious that she would look after her mother in this way. When she learned that her husband had told the counselor about her long daily visits, she asked the therapist if she was doing enough, and if not, what more she could do to help her mother. "After all, I am a nurse, so I should help my own mother, shouldn't I?" In therapy sessions, she often discussed the nursing staff at the facility, always concluding that "To them, it's just a bad job. After all, she's not their mother. Only I can give the kind of care she needs. It's the least I can do," she would add vehemently.

The counselor suspected that Sally's slavish devotion to her mother had strong undercurrents of a contradictory nature. Unlike the middle-aged son who could not face the changes in his ninety-two-year-old mother, Sally was not fearful of the signs of her mother's aging. On the contrary, she was ready to cater to them, with a vengeance.

The nursing home staff at first welcomed her as a caring relation and a competent colleague, but in almost no time at all they came to dread her visits. She would assess the state of the other patients in her mother's ward and immediately issue orders to the aides and orderlies. "Mrs. So-and-So has just soiled herself and needs to be changed," or "Mrs. What's-It needs a laxative." She so ruthlessly badgered her own mother with words, food, activity, and changes of clothing that the woman pleaded to be left alone.

The therapist, in exploring the dynamics of the family, learned that Sally's younger sister had died in her late teens. The mother deeply mourned her younger daughter's death; in her grief, she would tell Sally that she had lost her favorite child and no one could ever replace her. Thereafter, whenever Sally did anything that displeased her, the mother would begin to talk about the virtues of the sister.

Before her sister's death, Sally, then newly married, worked with her husband in his new business and enjoyed it.

After her sister's death, she decided to become a nurse. "I wanted my life to have more meaning. I felt I had to do something to help other people." The counselor noted in her talks with Sally's husband that he seemed to concur with much of what his wife had said, although he frequently ended his praise for her with wistful remarks about how he wished she would find more time to spend with him. Overall, though, he took a resigned attitude toward her "sacrifices, which are no more than every parent should expect from a good daughter."

Trying to Reverse the Past

Spontaneity, not affection, was lacking in the ways that Sally had regulated her home life and the lives of her husband and their two daughters, so that it was in every way the very opposite of her own early home life. "Dinner at six. We read them two stories before bedtime, and the children are asleep by seven." Nursing was chosen by her as a profession because it placed great emphasis on routine. Feeling exploited and unprotected, she could, in her profession, master her inner turmoil by a rigid routine and the offering of protection to others, thus protecting her own fears of vulnerability.

Psychotherapy uncovered Sally's deep ambivalent feelings of love and hate toward her mother, feelings she had never before allowed herself to recognize consciously, or to express. With help, she began to see that her overwhelming concern for her mother covered opposite feelings of dislike and resentment. Instead of accusing her mother of neglecting to give her the care and attention she had craved as a child, she now focused an overabundance of "care" onto her mother. Having felt enslaved by her own troubled emotions, she wanted to enslave her mother in a prison of caring.

As she gained insight into her behavior, Sally relinquished many compulsive actions toward her mother. She allowed the staff at the nursing home to do their job while she went back to part-time nursing. Visits to her mother gradually became less frequent, to everyone's relief. Sally became calmer and more relaxed with her mother. Communication between them seemed to become more direct, and some genuinely positive feelings developed as Sally, less driven by the fear of losing her mother's love, was able to be more flexible in her approach and risk the possibility of ambiguity—that is, of situations that were not so rigidly controlled and predictable. The older woman responded to this spontaneity and was able to reciprocate a little, as she was no longer so fearful of expressing her own dependency, lest her daughter respond with overcontrol as she had in the past.

Each individual and each family has a unique combination of dependent/independent needs. The ability to be one or the other at the appropriate time is crucial for successful living and aging. In our society, independence is overly stressed. The courage to stand alone is a greatly valued American virtue. From infancy, we are urged to stand on our own two feet, to always be in charge, to be self-reliant. In such an environment, it may take more strength to become dependent than to falter on alone. Conversely, throughout their lives, some people are overly demanding and dependent, and this pattern usually does not change as they grow older. The cues for accepting dependency lie in the older adult's ability to ask for help when this help is needed, while at the same time, not giving up awareness of themselves as separate people.

The Dependent Wife

After many years of marriage, a couple may have so totally shared ideas, actions, pleasures, friends, and experiences that they wonder how one could ever live without the other. Symbolically, they even seem to share one ego, one identity. Mary and John Largo were like that. They had been inseparable from the time they met as teenagers. They had married when John was in law school, and he often said he did not know how

The Family Ego and Adaptation to Change 21

he would have finished if Mary had not helped him with his studies, typed his papers, and encouraged him when he sometimes felt ready to quit. They chose not to have children, for they considered themselves to be most completely fulfilled as just the two of them. "He's my baby and I am his. We think, we breathe, we feel as one," Mrs. Largo said.

After forty years together, they began to have their first serious problems. Mrs. Largo, a slim, carefully groomed woman of seventy who looks at least ten years younger, explained to the therapist: "It all began about a year ago when John's assistant told me that several times he found him asleep at his desk during office hours. Can you believe it? Clients were waiting in the anteroom and he was sound asleep! It is so unlike him. When the assistant wakened him, John would be confused and sometimes didn't even know where he was. I did not see him behave this way for some months, so I thought the assistant was exaggerating. Then, during dinner one night, he said strange things I couldn't understand and he began to pace up and down in a funny way. I didn't know what to do, so I burst into tears and left the room."

Upon the advice of a friend, Mrs. Largo sought help for her husband, but not until several subsequent episodes had occurred in which this normally disciplined and mild-mannered man had acted in an uncontrollable and aggressive manner. One minute he seemed himself, and the next he became insulting and argumentative. Yet when his wife reproached him, it was obvious from his denials that he had no recollection at all of what he'd just done or said. Having become forgetful, he sometimes wandered for hours before he found his way home.

"We sit together as always, but now there's no one for me to talk to," Mrs. Largo said tearfully, demanding that the therapist do something or prescribe something to help him. "I cannot exist without him. How can he do this to me when we mean so much to one another?"

The therapist's first thrust was to help Mrs. Largo realize that her husband was not in control and that she would have to try to understand his unpredictable behavior. They discussed ways in which she could realistically cope with his condition. While a plan of treatment was drawn up for Mr. Largo, Mrs. Largo was also being helped to know herself. For over forty years she had been as one with her husband, inseparable from him, and now she had to take charge, to be a separate person and in a position of control.

Looking back over Mrs. Largo's life with her, she revealed that she was an infant when her mother died. Her father remarried soon after. He and his new wife were extremely devoted to one another, and while always kind to Mrs. Largo, they were perceived by her as mostly distant and aloof. Fearing repetition of the traumatic loss of her mother and the seeming rejection of her father, Mrs. Largo clung to her husband as the one person in the world who seemed to gratify her every wish. It was like finding her mother in him; she depended upon him just as the infant depends on its mother for survival. Changes in him felt like changes in herself, and his illness terrified and overwhelmed her.

"I have never had a thought, a secret, that I did not share with him. If he is not aware of me anymore, then for whom am I to dress, cook, and keep myself pretty? I live for him and through him," she said.

The therapist's task was to help her to become aware of her own needs and feelings, yet at the same time keep her sensitive to her husband's needs. The goal of treatment was to try to help her develop her own identity and inner resources so she could begin to function by herself and become responsible for her own future and her husband's. In clinical terms, the therapist's task was to try to help her individuate, to develop a sense of self as separate from others, as against merging and living only as part of another.

Aging and Self-Image

An eighty-three-year-old woman became very irritable during a family Christmas dinner because her grandson took her picture with his new Polaroid camera. On looking at it, she said, "You make me look like an old woman. Don't take my picture anymore." Such people simply deny that they are growing old. Others agonize over every wrinkle, sag, and gray hair, their own and sometimes their mate's. "I worry about whether I'll be turned on by my wife when her breasts get flabby," a young medical intern admitted during a lecture on aging and sexuality. Not to be "turned on" in later years was already feared, as were bodily changes associated with aging. Aging, he felt, would rob him of his sexuality and his underlying self-esteem. Fear of physical change, loss of power and total control over destiny are inherent in these attitudes. Beneath the seemingly superficial anxieties lie more complex and deeply embedded fears. They concern one's fear of annihilation, the terror of non-being; the fear of loss of love from an important person; fear of punishment (super-ego guilt) for past and present wrongs; and self-blame for allowing oneself to become old. These fears may originate early in life but, if not dealt with, may haunt us in later years.

An Awareness of Pain

The bonds that hold people together are essentially those of family. With its own unique history, each family, as each individual, over a period of time develops its own ego or perceptions of inner and outer realities. Exaggerated expectations created by the idealized scenes of life on television, in films, and in scores of "self-help" books may also contribute in some part to its psychological structure. In families where accomplishment is overly stressed and positive self-image depends largely upon such props as status, wealth, winning at games, or sexual conquests, signs of dependency and new needs for intimacy may not be easily tolerated. All the members may be so preoccupied with themselves that they cannot accommodate any deviation from the established norm, as when the mother—the pillar of strength—is not what she used to be and seems to be playing out a new role in her need for others. The stress that her dependency puts on them may lead to depression and self-blame, to pain turned inward rather than to reaching out to one another in shared feelings, trust, and cooperation. Established family patterns and lifelong rules are hard to change. The ability to face old age with equanimity and make the most of the time that is left is also an extremely difficult task; simultaneous with the need to be supportive of the aging parent, the middle-aged children also experience changes which need to be met and understood. Both generations may require special attention at precisely the same time.

These are the stark realities, and for family members to put the subject to the back of their minds and avoid discussing it merely turns the pain inward. Pain is a signal, and much anguish can be alleviated by recognizing what causes the pain and doing something about it. The family that is aware of its pain may suffer less than one that denies it.

Chapter Three

Senile Dementia

*Now all my singing Dreams are gone
But none knows where they are fled
Nor by what trail they have left me.*

Paiute Indian,
from "A Song In Time of Depression"

There are many physiological losses with age. The blood flow decreases. Hearing of high-pitched sound diminishes. We lose up to 50 percent of our sensitivity to taste and smell. Resistance to infection decreases and people become more susceptible to disease. There is a loss of tissue and vascular elasticity, and there are structural changes in the size of the brain. Throughout adult life, we lose brain cells at the rate of a small fraction of 1 percent per year, a loss not currently considered to be a crucial factor to brain function. Even if we were to lose twice the number of brain cells that we do each year, it is unlikely that our mental acuity would be significantly affected.

These physiological losses do not mean that after the age of sixty-five or seventy an individual will inevitably become deaf, will be short of breath, will no longer be able to enjoy sensory perceptions, and will become infirm and senile. Aging is synonymous with change, but it is not synonymous with sickness and senility.

Senility simply means "old age; the weakness and infirmity due to old age," yet the word has come to connote foolishness, impotency, and puerility, to name a few commonly used synonyms associated with it. In psychiatric circles, senility is often referred to as the wastebasket diagnosis for all the mental problems of the aged. Many behaviors that merely reflect individual differences in personality are often called senile, sometimes with tragic consequences. Elderly people suffering from such treatable disorders as vitamin deficiencies, tumors, anemia, depression, hyperthyroidism and other metabolic problems have been known to be dismissed and neglected because they were mistakenly classified as "hopelessly senile."

The disease that most closely resembles the stereotype of old age is called *senile dementia*. This refers to cognitive dysfunction manifested by loss of short-term memory, impaired judgment, and disorientation. More simply stated, individuals with senile dementia may have trouble remembering where they are, whether they are at home, in a neighbor's house, or in an institution. They may wander off and get lost, unable to find their way back. They cannot concentrate and often fail miserably at the simplest task. They may become withdrawn and cease to speak, or they may become angry and argumentative.

As people grow older, they may experience some memory deficits. Some degree of memory impairment is a characteristic and often common problem among the elderly. Decrements in short-term memory have been interpreted both in terms of reduced brain storage capacity and increased susceptibility to interference. Research scientists have attributed this to an overload of information, a theory that has to do with the actual location and amount of brain tissue available for the storage of new information. Because some memory problems may occur as a normal part of aging, this could be, and sometime is, confused with an attributed to early signs of memory loss in dementia.

The Stages of Dementia

Early Stages

In the early stages, memory problems usually involve disorientation toward time and place. Forgetting the names and ages of others occurs as the condition develops, but forgetting one's own name and other vital statistics is usually a more severe indication of dementia and occurs only in later stages.

However, there are other mental and physical impairments with dementia, particularly those related to activities of daily living (ADL). The demented are at risk because they become incapable of taking care of themselves. They forget to turn off the jets on their stoves, to lock doors, to dress appropriately for the weather, and to take medication. As the disease advances, they begin to look disheveled. If they live alone, their homes become dirty and disorganized. They cannot bathe themselves, wash their hair, or even comb it. Their sleeping habits may change, and they may wander in the night. There are rapid mood changes, from tears to laughter and vice versa. Loss of control of bowel and bladder may occur. Incontinence is frequently the last straw for those who take care of an elderly demented person living at home. It is often at this stage that care-givers find they can no longer cope with the responsibilities and seek admission to hospitals and nursing homes.

Final Stages

At the end, the victims of senile dementia are bedridden and noncommunicative. They may babble incoherently or not speak at all. Motor control is severely impaired. Some studies have found that the life expectancy of a demented person is less than one half that of a nondemented person of the same age. Even after controlling for age, higher death rates have been found for individuals with certain types of dementia. Often the cause of death is bronchopneumonia or other infection.

The ability to recognize the correct clues that lead to an accurate diagnosis is central to the art of healing. The early symptoms of measles, for instance, are a cold, a sore throat, a cough, and a rise in temperature. On the fourth day, a rash appears on the neck and behind the ears and gradually spreads to the rest of the body. If spots appear in any other form, or do not appear at all, the patient probably has not had the measles. Unfortunately, there are no such absolute clues or symptoms for determining dementia. There are, however, the classic core symptoms, described by Eric Pfeiffer (1978), a well-known geriatric diagnostician.

Classic Core Symptoms

- Disorientation toward person, place, and time
- Decreased short-term memory for recent events
- Difficulty in performing cognitive tasks related to spatial relations such as serial sequencing (recalling numbers forward and backward)
- In severe cases, difficulty with long-term memory for events long in the past

The *Diagnostic and Statistical Manual of Mental Disorders* (DSM-III), the handbook of symptoms published by the American Psychiatric Association, also includes impairment of intellectual functioning and emotional lability in its description of senile dementia. Emotional lability refers to inappropriate emotional outbursts of laughter, followed by crying for no apparent reason.

Types of Dementia

Sudden Onset Dementia

Different types of dementia with purportedly different clinical and organic characteristics are described in textbooks. The type that has been reported to account for about 20 percent of all dementias is that attributable to multi-infarcts or multiple strokes causing blood vessel disease in the brain. This has been called hardening of the arteries of the brain.

It is thought that this disorder is secondary to atherosclerotic disease. These dementias result from changes in the circulatory system, either from multiple blood clots restricting blood flow to the brain only, or to the entire body. In both cases, the blood supply to the brain is disturbed, causing disorientation, memory deficits, the inability to learn and calculate, and other symptoms similar to those of chronic dementia. Medical treatment may sometimes ameliorate the symptoms. Drugs that dilate the blood vessels and nourish the oxygen-starved brain tissue are prescribed.

Chronic Dementias

Senile dementia of the Alzheimer's type (SDAT) and Pick's disease were once thought to be a presenile psychosis, occurring between the ages of forty to sixty years. In Alzheimer's disease, the brain suffers widespread atrophy, whereas in Pick's disease, the degenerative changes are mostly confined to the frontal and temporal areas. Now, current evidence indicates that dementia of the Alzheimer's type (SDAT) characterizes fifty percent of all senile dementias. The physical abnormalities (identified with certainty through brain autopsy only), show shrinkage of individual nerve cells and the presence of senile plaques (decay), neurofibrillary tangles, and granulovacuolar degeneration. However, in another form of senile dementia called Jakob-Creutzfeldt's disease, there are no neural changes in the brain.

Although there are thought to be differences in the nature of brain cell lesions in these different types of dementia, the clinical symptoms are so similar, often occurring across disorders, that differentiation is extremely difficult while the victim is alive. Even the physical abnormalities, identified through brain autopsy, are often coincident. However, knowing that the patient has a history of strokes will aid the physician in diagnosis and treatment, because dementia caused by strokes may be reversible and rehabilitation often relieves the more acute symptoms.

If we were to look at a segment of the brain of a person who had symptoms of senile dementia, in many cases there would be brain atrophy and the presence of senile plaques and neurofibrillary tangles. The plaques are comprised of amyloid bodies. The neurofibrillary tangles are twisted filaments made up of protein. Curiously, not all people with dementia evidence these brain anomalies, and there are people with severely deteriorated brains who exhibit no signs at all of dementia. How these plaques and tangles develop, how they interfere with brain function, and how or if they can be treated once they occur are questions that biomedical researchers are trying to answer.

Causes of Dementia

Although there are many clues, there are also many contending theories about the causes. Among some commonly held theories are:

- Brain damage—resulting from hardening of the cerebrovascular arteries
- Heredity—may play a role
- Metabolic function—may cause biochemical abnormalities
- Brain cell loss—loss of nerve cells and synapses in the brain
- Strokes or multi-infarcts (dead sections of brain tissue)
- A slow-acting viral infection

The slow-acting viral infection theory is particularly hopeful because it suggests that someday a drug, perhaps even a vaccine, will be able to combat senile dementia.

It is still unclear what causes neuronal aberrations (why impulses from one brain cell to another are short-circuited). There is controversy over whether we are dealing with one disease entity with variants or with more than one disease. Scientists also debate over the genetic origins. The British research psychiatrist Sir Martin Roth believes there is evidence in favor of a polygenic theory of dementia, citing evidence from a number of Swedish studies showing higher rates of dementia among siblings of parents who also had been affected (Roth, 1980).

Incidence Rates

Reported rates of senile dementia vary, depending upon the type of epidemiological survey conducted, on the diagnostic techniques used, and the ways in which data are statistically analyzed.

- Overall estimates for individuals sixty-five and above range from 6.6 percent to 9 percent.
- Accepted prevalence rates for moderate to severe dementia in the community (noninstitutionalized) is between 4 percent and 7 percent (based on international studies such as Kay [1972] in England and Essen-Moller [1956] in Sweden). However, this figure differs among age groups. For instance, estimates for afflicted individuals under seventy-five years are less than 5 percent, but for those over eighty years, the prevalence rates have been estimated to be as high as 12 percent (Gurland et al., 1980).

It is also estimated that at least 50 percent of all patients (sixty-five and over) in long-term-care facilities are suffering from some type of dementia. The figures cited above for community-resident elderly refer to definite cases. If incipient or marginal cases are also included, then the rate becomes somewhat higher. Using a mathematical model for case detection, the rates may be as high as 9 percent for those sixty-five years and over living in the community (Golden, 1982).

If Golden's rates are accurate, it is clear that only a small minority of the older population suffer from the disorder, and that senile dementia is by no means synonymous or inevitable with old age. Nevertheless, small as the proportion may seem to be, the disease destroys the minds and the bodies of hundreds of thousands of victim a year, and extensive basic and clinical research is needed to combat these disorders.

*Individual Reactions
to the Onset of Dementia*

One individual's behavior and adaptation to the symptoms of dementia varies from another's depending upon personality and response style throughout life. Suspiciousness, paranoia, acute anxiety, panic, passivity, agitation, or hostility are some associative symptoms of dementia (Eric Pfeiffer, 1978).

A suspicious person is one who is very fearful of losing control. Therefore, such an individual will have an extremely severe reaction to losing the capacity to think clearly and to communicate. If the person has delusions, particularly of a paranoid nature, she* will react in a hostile way and suspect the motives of those who try to help her. It is very upsetting for relatives and friends who do not expect or anticipate such responses. For example, a young niece was visiting her aunt in a nursing home during lunchtime. They were having what the niece thought was a pleasant conversation when suddenly her aunt threw a glass of water in her face and scratched her arm. The niece had no idea of what she'd said to upset her aunt, who suffered increasingly from emotional lability in the advanced stages of senile dementia.

In nursing homes, where senile dementia affects a considerable number of the residents, misunderstandings can arise quickly and for seemingly little reason except that the individuals involved are very vulnerable, fearful of losing control, and therefore overly suspicious of others. For instance, it is not

*Where no sex difference is involved, we will mostly use feminine pronouns, for simplicity's sake and because there are more older women than older men in the United States.

unusual for a resident to misplace her handbag and then accuse a roommate of stealing it. Or a man may drape his sweater over the back of a chair and then wander off. He goes to another chair, thinking this is the chair he has just left, then becomes excited, accusing a staff member of stealing his sweater when he finds it missing.

Variables in Behavior

Just as individual responses to symptoms vary, the symptoms in each case may also vary. Sometimes they occur alone, sometimes in combination with other unusual symptoms. We describe a few of the more common symptoms to help the family member recognize the problems and degrees of impairment.

Perseveration

Dementia may affect the dominant temporal and lateral parietal regions on the right side of the brain. These control and affect the expressive and receptive use of language—that is, the way we understand and the way we talk. An individual may ramble incessantly, or use inappropriate word substitution as his speech becomes stereotypic or perseverative. For example, he may say, "I went to the ... the ... the ... the ... " and after some time, finally say, "the big box," which may mean that he went to the supermarket. These speech defects may occur with dementia; they may also frequently occur in people who suffer an acute trauma such as a stroke, a brain tumor, or a serious operation.

Agnosia and Apraxia

Agnosia is a disturbance in recognizing sensory impressions, such as simple objects: a key, a pencil, a comb. The individual may take a comb and begin to brush her teeth with it, or may not be able to recognize her own home. Identification of simple objects constitutes part of many diagnostic tests for severe dementia. A person with mild dementia can recognize simple objects. The severely impaired cannot. Physicians use this procedure as part of a standard workup for diagnosis.

Another symptom that characterizes dementia is *apraxia*, the inability to control motor tasks: making a fist, writing with a pencil, holding a fork.

Sudden onset dementia, caused by stroke or Parkinson's disease or other brain damage, may temporarily render the patient incapable of recognizing objects or using them appropriately. Depending upon what part of the brain has been damaged and how severely, there may also be difficulty with speaking, with remembering, and with muscle control. The onset of disabling symptoms is immediate in a stroke victim, but time and rehabilitation may restore some of these abilities, whereas the disabilities of chronic dementia develop gradually and become increasingly worse despite all efforts at rehabilitation.

Hiding the Signs

People in early stages of memory impairment become very tense and anxious when placed in situations requiring more cognitive skills than they think they can muster. Sometimes they try to hide the fact that they don't know an answer by reacting with great anger to simple questions. They may refuse to answer or insist that the question makes no sense. Others deny the problem though they give wrong answers. A woman of eighty-three consistently gave her age as fifty-five when asked how old she was, while another woman insisted she was born in August when her birth month was January.

Paranoid reactions should be distinguished from the natural fears that older people have of becoming senile. Because of society's attitudes about aging and senility, many older people are fearful of losing their mental capacities and of being thought of as senile by others. It is quite common to hear older people boast about their own mental acuity by favorably comparing themselves to the less fortunate. "Margaret, poor thing, doesn't even know her own daughter any more." In view of the terrible stigma attached to losing control of one's life, or of becoming dependent, or of "being put away," it is understandable that many older people—even those who know that senility is not an inevitable outcome in old age—sometimes live in fear of becoming a victim of this mind-destroying disease.

Since many people retain their social skills until quite late in the disease process and can compensate or cover up for their deficiencies, often the family doesn't become aware of the problem until something dramatic happens: Mother leaves the stove on all night; Dad drives the car off the road.

A common defense mechanism used by dementia victims is to answer questions in elaborate detail in order to impress others with their gift of conversation, or to obfuscate. A trained or a sensitive listener will notice that these long-winded answers never involve memory or cognition. If asked, "What year did your mother die?" the person will reply, "My mother was born in 1867 and was a very beautiful woman . . ." The individual will keep talking and become hurt or angry or anxious if the question is repeated.

As we have said, the onset of dementia is most often gradual. Warnings are usually subtle and not easily recognized. Unfortunately, this area has not yet been researched sufficiently to provide definite guides for diagnosis. Symptoms come and go at first. An individual has good days and bad days, making classification very difficult.

In the beginning there may be small personality changes. Irritability, increasing vacillation, occasional outbursts of temper, unexplained anger, or periods of withdrawal may occur, but not to the degree of frequency as to be alarming.

A daughter, for instance, is surprised when her mother suddenly becomes upset when she suggests they play canasta.

They had always played this card game during the daughter's annual visits home, so this unusual behavior could indicate that the mother has become fearful of showing her poor performance in the game, and chooses not to play at all.

The family is faintly aware that something is wrong, but can't quite determine what it is. Often, in retrospect, they will look back and recall that "Mom has not been herself for some time."

Subtle changes in intelligence take place. Victims are not as sharp as they once were. They have trouble making decisions and there are periods of forgetfulness. They may have difficulty doing more than one thing at a time, or may have delayed recall and tend to lose their train of thought easily. They may have problems understanding simple directions. Anxiety and/or depression can accompany these symptoms as the person begins to realize his or her deficits.

In making a diagnosis, it is extremely important to consider the individual's past personality and cognitive style. Some people have always had trouble following directions and always had a hard time remembering names. Therefore, it is change from past behavior that should be noted.

Mrs. Jackson was disciplined and precise in everything she did. Her daughter, Rae O'Brien, began to notice that her mother didn't seem as alert as usual and that for some time, perhaps a couple of years, the eighty-year-old woman was forgetting names and dates, but recalling in detail stories about summers they had spent in Maine over forty years before.

Mrs. O'Brien's son had several times mentioned that he thought Grandma was becoming senile, because she seemed to confuse him with his cousin. Mrs. O'Brien got angry with him for talking like that, although she was becoming a bit suspicious when, on two separate occasions, her mother completely forgot about regular doctor's appointments and then angrily accused the receptionist of making a mistake. This was very unusual behavior for a woman who was known never to be late for an appointment. The family physician did tests and said he thought that she had incipient dementia.

Clinical Assessment of Functional Capacity

An older individual who is having trouble coping to the point where day-to-day living is troublesome to herself and to her family is clearly in need of some form of assessment, preferably by a clinical geriatric team. The team may include physicians of all specialties, nurses, social workers, or others involved in health-care delivery services. Recently centers have been established across the country to expedite the coordination of disciplines in executing gerontological research and in providing clinical services to the elderly. The centers are affiliated with major teaching and medical research facilities. However, it is important to note that these diagnostic centers are still in the early stages of development and their services are not yet readily available to the general public. Most people still must rely on family physicians for assessment, on social workers in hospitals, or on nurses affiliated with visiting nurse service agencies. The training and sensitivity of these individuals to problems specific to the elderly is variable, and it is advisable that before seeking advice, the family should make sure that the person they approach and hire actually has experience with older people.

In a clinical workup, typically both the older person and the family are interviewed to determine the extent of the problem and to draw up plans for further and more extensive assessment, if necessary. The family member may be asked to respond to questions about the following areas of function. (Many of these items are taken from a measure designed by Blessed, Tomlinson, and Roth, 1968, to assess mental functioning, and from a measure of functional capacity designed by Katz et al., 1970).

Cognitive Functioning

Does the older person have difficulty in the following areas?

1. Dealing with money or making change.
2. Remembering short lists such as grocery items needed from the store.

3. Finding her way around the house.
4. Finding her way around the neighborhood.
5. Recognizing where she is, with whom she is residing, and with whom she is in contact. In other words, can the person recognize different family members and friends?
6. Recalling immediate events such as a television program that has just ended, appointments with doctors, dates, and the like.

Personality Changes

Has there been a noticeable change in the following areas? Has the older person recently shown *increasing* signs of the following?

1. Rigidity in thinking and behavior.
2. Irritability, petulance, and/or inability to control emotions.
3. Self-involvement to the point of ignoring others.
4. Flattening of affect; for example, showing little or no excitement or enthusiasm over celebrations or events which in the past had elicited such responses.
5. Hyperactivity.
6. Apathy.
7. Sexually inappropriate behavior (masturbating in public).

Have there been noticeable *decreases* in the following areas?

1. Concern for others. A decrease may be noticed in the person's tact, insight, and in concern about the feelings of others.
2. A decline in hobbies and interests.
3. Diminished sexual drive.
4. Less initiative in solving problems and making decisions.

It is important to realize that some of these changes may occur with normal aging or due to life events. Not all of these personality changes will be present in any one person, and the significance of any combination of these symptoms requires a careful examination of possible causes other than incipient dementia.

Activity Limitation

The family member may also be asked if the older person has difficulty performing tasks necessary for day-to-day living (ADL). Inability to perform these activities may indicate medical or psychiatric disorders or both:

1. Eating
    - Can the person feed herself without assistance or is she very sloppy when no help is given?
    - Does the person need help in opening cartons, in cutting food?
    - Does the person require someone to feed her?
2. Dressing
    - Is the person able to dress without difficulty?
    - Is minor assistance needed with zippers and buttons, or will they remain unzipped and unbuttoned if no help is given?
    - Does the person need major assistance such as help with most articles of clothing (shoes, socks, underwear) that must be put on the person?
3. Household tasks. Are tasks such as laundry, shopping, cleaning, bill paying, and handling business affairs done without difficulty, or are there problems such as:
    - The person can wash only a few items of hand laundry.
    - The person can walk only two blocks to a local store for a few grocery items, but these items are insufficient for her needs.
    - Dishes remain unwashed due to inability.

Continence (Bladder and Bowel)

Does the person occasionally have an accident where she wets herself, perhaps at night, less than once a week, or are accidents more frequent, as often as several times a week?

Other more detailed questions might be asked of the family (or of the older person if she is capable of responding) to assess needs for services and care as well as to determine precisely what family members are able and willing to do to help out.

Psychiatric Diagnostic Techniques

An older person who is mentally capable will be directly asked about her functioning with questions similar to those addressed to family members, as listed in the preceding pages. If it is suspected that the older person is suffering from dementia, then a mental status test is frequently added to the assessment. A well-known measure which is usually included as part of a psychiatric examination is the Mental Status Questionnaire (MSQ), popularized by Dr. Robert Kahn and Dr. Alvin Goldfarb (1960). It has long been part of traditional psychiatric interviews given to determine memory impairment; it contains many items originally compiled by Sir Martin Roth and his colleagues in England.

The MSQ is a brief, ten-item measure. The patient is asked to give his name, date of birth, address, what is the date and day of the week, who is the President of the United States, and the like. Simple as it may seem, the measure taken from the answers is useful in separating the clearly mentally impaired from those with few or no symptoms of retardation. However, it is a screening device only and is not sensitive in detecting early dementia or in closely examining the more severely impaired. Disorientation toward person, place, and time are symptoms of schizophrenia and other psychotic disorders as well as of dementia. Therefore, anyone placed in a psychiatric emergency room would be asked questions similar to those contained in the Mental Status Questionnaire (MSQ).

Besides th MSQ, there are a number of other indicators that may be included in an assessment of cognitive functioning. For example, a person may be asked to demonstrate the ability to count, make change, or remember a series of numbers (digit spans). Specifically, some diagnosticians will ask the person to count to twenty by twos, subtract three from thirty and keep subtracting the number three all the way to zero or to remember a string of several numbers. Another behavioral item involves placing coins in front of the individual and asking her to give the interviewer a specified amount. Several standard assessment screens exist, but many clinicians use their own versions, which contain variations or subsets of the standard measures.

Other means of testing for primary and secondary symptoms of dementia include psychometric and neurometric tests of learning ability and recall. Examples of psychometric tests are the Wechsler Adult Intelligence Test (WAIS) and the Minnesota Multiphasic Personality Inventory (MMPI).

Medical Diagnostic Techniques

Whenever disturbing symptoms occur, the older person should be given a thorough physical examination to determine whether the causes may be of a reversible origin, such as tumors, infection, thyroid imbalance, or drug reactions. Along with the traditional components of a medical examination (chest X rays, laboratory tests, electrocardiogram, and so forth), there should also be a careful survey of all prescribed and over-the-counter medications the person is taking. More specific tests may then be recommended.

Since the early 1960s, techniques have been developed to produce views of the workings of the human brain. A number of these techniques are being used to screen for physical evidence of dementia, but they are not completely free from complications dangerous to the patient, nor have they yet had a high success rate in detecting the structural changes necessary for accurate diagnosis. They include:

- Skull X ray, which is examined for evidence of intracranial calcification.
- Angiograms, X rays to show the flow of blood to see if there is fatty degeneration or hardening and narrowing of the arteries.
- Electroencephalogram (EEG), used for detection of the characteristically slow, disorganized brain waves of a person with dementia. In this test, the oxygen consumption and the blood flow to the brain are studied to observe decreases that are characteristic of dementia.
- Computerized axial tomography, known as the CAT scan, has been used in recent years to photograph successive slices of the brain for anomalies. The CAT scan of the brain produces a detailed image that can show the location of tumors or blood clots. This image is made when a moving pencillike beam of X rays is passed through the head to detect subtle differences in tissue density.
- Positron emission tomography, or the PET scan, is being used in medical diagnosis, particularly in clinical brain research. In PET scanning, a radioactively labeled fluid is injected into the patient's bloodstream and the emissions are recorded on a screen. Millions of recordings are made for a given section of the brain and then analyzed by computer. PET scanners may be used to study strokes, multiple sclerosis, and Huntington's disease.

Mistaken Diagnoses

Differentiating between senile dementia and other disorders or problems is not easy, but there are some helpful criteria to consider. Sir Martin Roth notes that in the Newcastle study, individuals were incorrectly diagnosed as suffering from early or incipient dementia when it turned out later that they were in a severe state of depression (Nunn et al., 1974). Incorrect diagnoses occurred more frequently among women than men. Roth (1978) also states that the onset of dementia is gradual, that it takes from five to ten years to develop to a severe stage, that it is more likely to begin after the age of seventy to seventy-five; that memory impairment is always present, and that frequently there are accompanying personality changes. For instance, an individual considered mild-mannered for most of his life suddenly becomes brusque and abrasive in many situations; or a person with many interests and friends suddenly becomes withdrawn and depressed.

Too often it is assumed that the symptoms of depression are harbingers of senility, with the result that older people are needlessly institutionalized and then neglected because their condition is thought to be chronic and untreatable.

Drug intoxification is a common cause of mistaken diagnosis. The elderly are often multimedicated. An older person may have diabetes, angina, and arthritis, and take a different medication for each ailment. Having to take several pills at regular intervals every day can lead to mistakes in taking the correct dosage at the right time; and errors will be greater among older people whose eyesight may be failing and who may be in a weakened or confused state.

However, there are other reasons for drug intoxification, apart from mistakes on the part of the older person in following physicians' directions. The aged are more susceptible to adverse effects from medication than are younger people. Aging affects changes in metabolism, excretion, tissue binding, and organ responsiveness. The proportion of fat cells, in which some drugs accumulate, also increases with age. Therefore, drugs are absorbed and retained at a different rate depending upon age, while the drug manuals that doctors refer to when prescribing medication are geared toward middle-aged people. Also, certain drugs—those prescribed for high blood pressure, for instance—may produce a depressive reaction.

The physician's attitude toward older people may contribute to drug intoxification. As Dr. Robert Butler, the former director of The National Institute on Aging and chairman of the Department of Geriatric Medicine at Mt. Sinai Medical School, New York City, wrote in his book, *Why Survive:*

> Since the advent of psychoactive drugs in the 1950s, tranquilizers and anti-depressants have become widely used in the care of older patients. These drugs are frequently given as much for the tranquility of the institution or the physician as for the comfort of the patient. On an out-patient basis, general practitioners and psychiatrists find that psycho-active agents are an easy answer for the many complicated physical and emotional reactions of late life. It is much simpler to give a pill than to listen to complaints. (pp. 198-199)

The taking of any one or a combination of drugs may not necessarily lead to drug intoxification nor be mistaken for dementia, but if the onset of unusual symptoms occurs coincidentally with starting a new drug regimen, this should be noted.

Pseudodementias

Recent research indicate that one half of all senile dementia is due to Alzheimer's disease. The remainder consists of multi-infarct (stroke), Pick's disease, and other types of diseases. Studies also note that as high a rate as 12 percent of all older people suffering from problems with symptoms similar to those of dementia were mistakenly diagnosed as being chronically demented. A partial list of illness that may cause dementia-like symptoms include:

- Tumors, in the brain and elsewhere.
- Some cardiovascular diseases that reduce blood supply to the brain.
- Vitamin deficiencies, often involving B_{12} or folic acid.
- Infections that can exist in the elderly without fever or raised white blood cell count.

- Metabolic problems such as hyperthyroidism, chronic renal (kidney) failure, chronic liver failure.
- Ingestion of toxins such as mercury or lead.
- Reactions to drugs such as neuroleptics (antipsychotics used for treatment of disorders such as schizophrenia), antidepressants, anticonvulsants (Dilantin), and digitalis.

These disorders are known as pseudodementia or reversible dementia, because the causes can be treated and the symptoms ameliorated.

Treatment

Older people suffering from dementia, and their families, are naturally eager for some sort of treatment, but no known cure has yet been found for chronic senile dementia. There are some drugs on the market that manufacturers claim will reduce confusion and disorientation. These medications will not significantly reduce the symptoms or the progression of the disease, but they may have some ameliorative affects, such as reducing anxiety for the agitated patient.

Recently, excitement has been generated over the potential benefits of a food substance called choline for the treatment of dementia. Choline is usually found in eggs, soybeans, and liver, as well as in lecithin, a food additive. Choline stimulates brain cells to produce more acetylcholine, a substance that transmits nerve impulses. We know that memory impairment is present when impulses from one brain cell to another are short-circuited, although it is not yet clear what causes these aberrations. Since the discovery in 1975 at Massachusetts Institute of Technology (MIT) that choline has a prompt effect on the brain's ability to produce acetylcholine, the substance has been used experimentally to treat Alzheimer's disease, manic-depressive illness, and other diverse conditions.

Choline is one of the few substances able to penetrate the so-called blood-brain barrier, which scientists generally believe protects the brain from direct influences of a daily diet intake with too much or not enough of a balance of nutrients. Until these experiments were done, only alcohol and narcotics were thought to be able to penetrate the blood-brain barrier.

Research has shown that demented individuals have less than normal amounts of choline in their brains, and in research trials with only a small number of subjects, results showed improved memory scores. These trials were conducted by Drachman and associates at Northwestern University, and by Wurtman at MIT.

Wurtman reported recently that he and his colleagues have been able to increase performance on objective tests of memory for 30 percent of the subjects after giving large amounts of phosphatidylcholine, a choline compound which is found in cell membranes (Wurtman, 1980). Dr. Wurtman cautions that a person would have to eat about forty-eight eggs a day to have any appreciable effect, and adds that choline available over the counter as a dietary supplement is not in the proper form or dose to produce the desired memory improvements. It should be emphasized that at this time there is no real remedy for the symptoms of dementia and that, hopeful as it may seem, this particular research is still in the experimental stages.

Family Involvement in Treatment

Often the physician is very concerned about the distress of the patient and the family, and will prescribe medication on the outside chance that it will help. Many physicians were taught medicine under the medical model, which is a cure model. This makes them feel that they are failing the patient and the family if they cannot do something to cure or at least alleviate the symptoms. The family can help in this situation by remaining open for candid discussion with the physician about the problem; they should let the physician know they do not expect miracle cures where none exist.

The family should be vigilant. If they notice anxiety, forgetfulness, or apathy in older relatives, they should try to find out what is bothering them. Many reasons other than organic brain disorder can produce these symptoms among the elderly. Loneliness, anxiety about the health of a close friend or a spouse, concern about their own health, sadness over a recent death, financial insecurity, fears about coping alone in case of illness are all among the realities with which older people must live on a day-to-day basis. Sometimes the course of an illness or an emotional problem will not change for the better, and the older person cannot find a way to adjust to it alone. It is then that the family needs to assess the problem and define its role as care-giver.

Chapter Four

Behavioral Problems

*Since I am convinced
That Reality is in no way
Real,
How am I to admit
That dreams are dreams?*

Saigyo Hōshi (from *Seven Poems*)

In the preceding chapter we discussed organic brain disorders and chronic senile dementia. We cited some of the various conflicting theories concerning their causes and their treatment as well as the difficulties involved in distinguishing between irreversible chronic dementias and the treatable pseudodementias.

In this chapter we will deal specifically with functional disorders or disturbed behaviors that appear to be related to the individual's personality and life experiences, and will discuss how clinicians and the family can cope with these problems.

A wide range of mental and emotional conditions tends to afflict the elderly, but it should be noted that many of these conditions and symptoms are also common to younger people who are under stress. Emotional disturbances are present not because most old people are senile. Rather they represent the complexity of problems and experiences which human beings bring to old age because of the ways in which adaptation to changing situations and the process of aging may affect their responses. These problems and conditions need to be studied free from fear and prejudice, for if properly treated, they can sometimes be cured, or their painful symptoms can at least be somewhat alleviated.

Emotional Disturbances

There is no short or simple definition of what constitutes disturbed behavior. A broad definition of disturbed behavior would include: a deviation from the usual stable pattern of behavior that is consistent with an individual's personality. Very often, changes in normal patterns of behavior must be perceived for clinical purposes as disturbed: An ordinarily quiet, reticent, and mild-mannered man suddenly, and with regular frequency, becomes quarrelsome, litigious, and combative. In the broader perspective, argumentative or litigious behavior would not necessarily be perceived as abnormal, but for this individual the sharp change in behavioral style may well need to be seen as abnormal. The family or the clinician should then ask what has accounted for the change. A thorough checkup by a physician is always a sensible first step.

How a particular family tolerates different or deviant behavior is another consideration. For instance, in a 1960s hippie-type commune, the wearing of love beads, long hair, and jeans, and the open smoking of marijuana would not be seen as unusual, but in a small middle-American town it would be considered inappropriate and perhaps even abnormal. However, some families, regardless of the life-style they follow, are more tolerant of deviant behavior than others. Clinicians routinely encounter patients who have been eccentric in their behavior for some time before they were brought for consultation. In these cases, inevitably there is a particular incident or situation which suddenly changes the family's perception of that person from eccentric to sick and disturbed.

Attitudes usually change when older people act in ways that are dangerous to themselves or to family members, such as becoming aggressive and abusive, refusing to take needed medication, driving a car when they do not have sufficient control of it. The clinician must then incorporate some sense of a threshold, and in particular, *the* threshold of tolerance for those closely related to a disturbed older person who is at risk and whose actions may endanger others.

Disturbed behavior is a translation of unsettled and troubled thinking which people in emotional pain express in many different ways. There is no Richter scale of 1 to 10 for measuring emotional pain, but certain characteristic symptoms are indicative. However, no one sign or symptom is definitive. Many examples of cause and effect are needed to begin a proper diagnosis.

People in emotional pain, and in physical pain as well, may become almost hopelessly self-obsessed. Self-obsession may be the manifestation of an instinct for survival, but it may be acted out in ways that are very difficult for others to tolerate. One minute troubled individuals are struggling internally, the next moment they may do or say things that under normal circumstances they themselves would consider inexcusable. They may withdraw and develop socially isolating behavior, or may become hypersexual. They may become confused or perplexed and lose their sense of reality and judgment. They may become aggressive and assaultive. Their mood states may swing from elevated to depressed. They may believe that strangers are persecuting them. Among older people it is not unusual to find that sometimes more than one of these conditions exist at a time.

Affective Disorders

Depression

Affective disorders refer to emotional problems involving mood, and include both manic disorders, characterized by elation and euphoria, and depression. The following discussion will focus on depression because it is the most prevalent type of emotional disorder in the elderly. It is both a symptom of a temporary mood and a psychiatric category of diagnosis. At some time in their lives, almost everyone has experienced demoralization as a natural response to significant changes or events: the breakdown of a relationship, the loss of a loved one or a job, financial problems, or fears about aging. These feelings turn into a depressed state when the periods of sadness, pessimism, and uncertainty become prolonged and so overwhelming that they affect judgment, concentration, and cognitive ability. Clues to the depth of its seriousness are evidenced by apathy, loss of pleasure, negative expectations, and an exaggerated view of problems. Symptoms vary and may also include increased dependence, loss of motivation, physical problems such as loss of appetite, overeating, insomnia, loss of sexual interest, and somatic complaints such as headaches, dizziness, and stomach pains without medical basis. In extreme cases, depression can lead to suicidal ideation or wishes.

Stress is a common cause of depression. As people grow older they seem to have fewer reserves with which to overcome the effects of stress. Thus, depression is a serious problem among the elderly, often producing a significant slowdown or a significant acceleration of their motor activity, which gives rise to *anxiety* and *agitation*.

Anxiety causes excessive worrying, ruminative and repetitive thoughts. *Agitation* leads to pacing, finger and foot tapping, and other irritating motor mannerisms. Anxiety is a subjective experience of disquiet and distress, and though agitation expresses itself as a motor restlessness, it may also involve pressure of thoughts and speech.

Depressed people make others feel tense and nervous and so risk becoming socially isolated. Their attitude of utter helplessness makes their companions feel helpless as well. Every positive statement one can make to them is countered by their negative responses: "What's the use?" "It's no good at all!" "It's a waste of time!"

Their conversation is filled with statements of self-denigration: "I'm no good at all" or "I never could do that," indicating their utter lack of self-esteem, which is a basic part of their problem. It should be noted that an individual in a profound state of mourning differs from this picture of depressed behavior in that there is little or no self-reviling or self-reproach or a fall in self-esteem in grief.

Among older people, the depressive condition is often hard to diagnose because it is difficult to distinguish between behaviors indicative of affective disorders and those that are the result of organic brain damage. Also, older people are subjected to many real stresses: retirement, changes in physical appearance and social status, sensory losses, widowhood, and the death of close friends, colleagues, and relatives. Often, if something is done to make life more tolerable for them, their depression may be alleviated.

It is important for family members attempting to help an older relative to recognize the distinction between demoralization and depression. Demoralization is usually more reactive—that is, a reaction to loss of others or to environmental stressors such as chronic illness, fear of crime in their changing neighborhood, and lack of social interactions. Demoralization is usually a less severe disorder than depression, but the prevalence rates are higher. (Estimates range from 20 to 30 percent of noninstitutionalized individuals over sixty-five years of age.) Jerome Frank, a noted psychiatrist, has defined demoralization as a state commonly associated with the following symptoms:

Nervousness/Anxiety: feels fidgety, tense; admits to worrying about many things or almost everything; bothered by feelings of restlessness; is more irritable than usual.

Somatic Complaints: describes headaches, stomach discomfort, general malaise; fears getting ill; poor appetite in absence of medical condition; suffers cold sweats, acid stomach, constipation; hands tremble; feels shaky.

Sadness: feeling blue; feels in low spirits; feels like crying; feels lonely.

Hopelessness/Helplessness: feels that nothing turns out right; feels helpless; has little hope for future; worried/pessimistic about future.

Poor Self-Esteem: feels useless, compared to other people of same age; feels she is not as good; not satisfied with self as a person; blames self for past/present behavior; doesn't feel she has much to be proud of.

Helping the Depressed Person

A great deal of patience is required when responding to the suffering of a depressed person. Sometimes all one can do is sympathize and acknowledge the individual's sense of loss. If she responds at all, you may suggest some ways to compensate.

Clinical depression, on the other hand, is a more serious condition; the prevalence rates for this condition are lower than for demoralization (estimates are from 2 to 15 percent). Often severe depression is a lifelong problem. An individual who is depressed may suffer some of the same symptoms as those described as demoralized. However, a depressed person will also experience some or all of the following. According to the *Diagnostic and Statistical Manual of Mental Disorders* (DSM-III), the individual must experience four of the following categories of symptoms in order to be considered clinically depressed:

Suicidal Thoughts: considered or tried suicide in the past month (in an assessment of the present condition).

Severe Sleep Difficulty: has sleep disorder due to tension, altered mood; has early morning awakening; sleeps too much.

Weight Change: losing weight (one pound a week) or not eating well in absence of medical problem or dieting.

Loss of Energy: is especially slow in morning; very tired.

Loss of Interest in Activities: has enjoyed little lately; loss of enjoyment in recreation due to depression, nervousness.

Feelings of Self-Blame: blames self for past or present behavior.

Inability to Concentrate: indecisive, slow-thinking.

Feelings of Doom: future seems bleak/unbearable; has not been happy in past month; has been seriously depressed prior to past month. In order for a person to be classified as more than mildly depressed, the person must either be suicidal or experience at least three of the following symptoms: weight loss, early morning awakening, mood worse in morning, excessive guilt, loss of interest in usual activities. A severely depressed person will be unable to function (go to work, care for the house, clothe and feed herself). A person who is moderately to severely depressed requires professional intervention, and anyone who speaks of suicide should be taken seriously.

Another distinction, beside that between depression and demoralization, is that between depression and the "complaining syndrome." Some older people tend to complain a great deal about how they feel and what they are worrying about in an effort to get others to listen and pay attention to them. This may be a lifelong habit or it may develop as the result of loss of a loved one, having fewer activities than in the past, or because of a diminished ability to get outside the home frequently enough. As expressed in many of our example cases, the cause of the complaining should be examined to see if such simple remedies as increased visits or other activities could help to make the individual feel more loved and involved.

If a woman says that for a few moments she had some pleasure, perhaps from watching a television program or the visit of a grandchild, then talk about these pleasures, no matter how rarely they occur. Reinforce every sign of self-acceptance by saying, "You should enjoy yourself; you deserve to. . . . You should find more ways to get pleasure." Depressives need to feel warmth and compassion from those around them, not projections of guilt and blame.

When depression is acute, this may not seem to help at all, but it is a more positive approach then saying, "I can't understand why you are so depressed" or "I can't understand why you are talking like that, you have so much to be thankful for."

Instead, tell the person, "I understand how you feel . . . I feel badly for you and would like to help you." It is no palliative to remind the depressed person that the patient in the next bed is worse off and really has something to be depressed about. These statements may appear as rejecting to the older depressed person and serve only to intensify feelings of guilt, self-blame, humiliation, and self-hate.

The Wish to Die

The wish to die is very strong among the severely depressed and is likely to be the underlying cause of suicide among older people. Suicide rates among men increase progressively from ages fifteen to eight-five. Although there is no sudden surge of suicide at any age, the rate is at its peak for men over the age of seventy-five. And it is believed that the actual number of elderly suicides is much higher than the reported figures because families, out of guilt, shame, or both, are frequently unwilling to report suicide as a cause of death. It is also acknowledged that the aged can kill themselves in ways that are not easily detected. They can kill themselves passively, by intentionally failing to take life-sustaining medication or by drinking too much and eating too little.

Alcoholism and starvation lead to slow deaths that are not without signs of warning, if only someone will notice, but it may be only after the fact that neighbors and relatives ask in wonder and dismay, "Why did he do it?" Of course there are many reasons, but sometimes an older man, living alone in a populous urban environment, feels totally abandoned. His wife has died. His children live far away. His work life is ended. Many friends are also gone. He has nothing to do but take care of his own needs, but he is tired all the time and so neglects to look after himself. Even his past is diminishing because he has no one with whom to recall the good times, and so his memory begins to fail. Living alone, afflicted with inactivity and with nothing to look forward to in the future, he sinks into apathy and a slow death.

Male suicide rates are higher than female suicide rates at all ages and in all countries for which there is adequate data to compute these figures. Yet women are known to suffer more from depression than men, and more often to make gestures of attempted suicide, particularly during their middle years when the children leave home and when they may be experiencing some depressive effects from the hormonal changes they undergo during menopause. However, menopause does not in itself cause debilitation, except in about 10 percent of women, and as more women enter the work force, the adjustment from fulltime to part-time motherhood is becoming easier. It may be that cultural attitudes affect some women in their middle years. If, for instance, a woman equates youth and fertility with sexuality, then menopause may be a devastating blow to her self-esteem, as she may believe that it strips her of her identity as a sexual and worthwhile being. The ability to overcome these stresses in their middle-years may provide women with the resilience to survive losses and deficits in later life.

The male sense of identity usually faces its most devastating tests of status and power loss at the time of retirement and through fear of sexual impotence at a more advanced age, and some men may not have the resilience or inner resources to withstand these crises in their later years. For both men and women, there seems to be an inverse relationship between sexual experience and depression (Blum and Weiner, 1979).

In the past few years, researchers have been looking for reasons for the higher rates of suicide among elderly men. Among some issues they are considering are the following: Are women less inclined to self-destruction, or are they less successful at accomplishing it? (A really determined act of self-destruction is not easy to accomplish.) Data shows more attempts among women and more success among men. When men choose to commit suicide, they use more foolproof methods. Are women more successful at using a suicide attempt as a plea of help, whereas men are unable to ask for help this way and instead actually kill themselves? Is suicide among older men related to their tendency to mismanage medication? Is it related to a reluctance to accept physical dependency?

Somatic Disorder

Hypochondriasis

Many depressed people get into an anxiety state about their health and suffer from imaginary ills. They are in a constant search for help and frequently visit their doctors with demands for medication and even hospitalization. They worry about their bodies, or some part of their bodies which they believe to be diseased. The pain and discomfort are no less real because they are due to emotional concerns and are not of physical origin. Hypochondriacs live in a permanent state of panic about their health. At a point of acute severity, they may writhe in pain, have difficulty with breathing, vomit, run a high temperature. They may stop eating, or the condition may be so severe that they are no longer able to digest food; the lack of nourishment may, in extreme cases, cause death.

Cognitive Disorders

Aging and its accompanying stresses can affect cognitive thinking as well as mood. A severely depressed individual may be unable to think logically or to concentrate long enough to remember what she is told. In such an individual, poor judgment is just as much a warning sign as fever is in a sick child. *Poor or impaired judgment* refers to a very low level of decision making, which most people do efficiently and without serious thinking when their judgment is intact. For instance, a man with failing eyesight and a heart condition is warned not to drive his car anymore, yet he persists in doing so. A woman who is disoriented in time and space gets up in the middle of the night to visit her daughter who has, in fact, moved away from the neighborhood.

There is a strong indication of cognitive defects when a person does things and is unaware of doing them. Before improvement can be expected, the patient must first become aware of her defects.

Loss of Reality Testing

Since many things in life lend themselves to interpretation, one's ability to perceive reality in much the same way as others perceive reality is highly subjective and sometimes quite subtle. However, in the broad, dramatic sense there are certain clearcut markers, as the following comparison points out:

Consider two older women, each living on her own. The first one, aged seventy-seven, talks incessantly about the "evil ones" who are coming to get her. She has many locks on her front door and is loathe to open the door unless she is sure that it is a friend on the other side. She burns her lights all night, is frightened when she goes out and when she is at home alone. It would be easy to diagnose her as a paranoid schizophrenic with delusional symptoms if we didn't know of the circumstances that influence her behavior. She lives alone in a high-crime neighborhood and has already been a victim of muggings and break-ins.

The second women, also in her late seventies, is very sociable, still active in charities, drives a car, and lives in much the same comfortable style she did all her life. She is widowed and sadly acknowledges the death of her husband, some ten years before, but then goes on to say that he comes to visit and drinks tea with her every afternoon.

The careful listener will become aware of the differences between these two responses. One is a response reflecting the best of a way of life that would tax the most resilient. It is consistent with the reality of the times. The second woman denies a reality, her husband's death, and lives with this unreal thought.

Paranoid Disorders

Some older people may develop persecutory ideas. These ideas may refer to neighbors, family members, or to strangers, and generally involve erroneous notions of hostile intent. It is not altogether clear why latent character traits flower later in life, but it is theorized that paranoid syndromes in the elderly are essentially derived from cognitive (intellectual) defect and an effort to explain phenomena or events which are otherwise not understandable. All people need to explain to themselves what they cannot understand or control. To be considered normal, these explanations fall within a generally accepted sense of reality. Not having a clear grasp of this reality, the parnoid person seizes upon seemingly bizarre explanations of a phenomenon. The explanation, albeit maladaptive, is nevertheless an explanation for them. However, you have to establish or reestablish a trusting, predictable relationship with a paranoid person and, through conversation, be careful not to become incorporated into her plot. Do not dispute her explanations, which will only make her more defensive, but at the same time do not limit conversation to topics that will arouse paranoid ideas. Change the subject entirely by initiating talk on other matters.

The decrements or losses in sensory ability which are often a part of growing old may be a reason for the development of paranoid ideas. When sight and hearing are impaired (and hearing more than sight) there seems to be a tendency to develop paranoid ideas. This is also true of younger people. Anecdotal evidence from nursing homes indicates that paranoid suspiciousness becomes heightened when residents' hearing aids are lost or misplaced. As soon as the hearing aids are recovered and used again, suspiciousness diminishes dramatically.

There is a significant difference between the paranoid syndromes of the elderly and the paranoid symptoms associated with the mental illness *schizophrenia*. Schizophrenia typically has its onset in late adolescence or early adulthood and may commonly have paranoid delusions among its symptoms. There are many forms of schizophrenia and many differences in its severity. A history of breakdowns over the course of a person's life may suggest schizophrenia or other mental illnesses. However, if paranoid syndromes first develop in middle or late life, then schizophrenia is almost certainly not the correct diagnosis.

Psychoses and Primitive Impulses

The following symptoms are rare among the elderly and occur most frequently with severe stages of dementia or in the psychotic elderly. You would not see these symptoms among most normal older people, just as you would not see them often among most normal younger people.

Most people adhere to standards of behavior that are generally recognized as socially acceptable. However, inadequate or deteriorated defenses can sometimes cause the loss of awareness of simple social expectations and create an uncontrollable sense of urgency to fulfill basic needs and desires. For instance, an elderly person invited to a party expresses childlike impatience while waiting to be served. The impulse or desire to be nourished breaks through socially accepted behavior.

At a more advanced stage of senile dementia, impulsive breakthroughs can occur with public displays of urination, defecation, and masturbatory and other hypersexual behaviors. Sometimes there is a verbal outpouring or outrageous statements as well. These statements seem to come out of the unconscious, which does not distinguish between what is said and what is thought. Sometimes the older person may behave in a rational way, but suddenly speak outrageously and out of context. When confronted with their unacceptable behaviors, they will seem to have no actual memory of what they have said and done, and will deny everything.

Perseveration

The tendency to repeat a set of ideas over and over again is called *perseveration*. It is a common aspect of disturbed brain function in all ages, not just among the elderly or the demented. In severe cases, a woman who perseverates will do a task correctly, such as combing her hair, but then continue doing it for an inordinately long time, even if a new task is being asked of her.

In less severe cases, perseveration may be manifested by telling the same story over and over, with no recollection of having told the story before. *Perseveration* must be differentiated from an obsessive or a ruminative idea, which is the tendency to repeatedly worry about something. For instance, John was with a friend when the friend died. There was a glass of water on the friend's bedside table. John did not give his friend the water, and now thinks that he would have saved his friend's life if he had. "He would still be alive today if only I had given him some water," John repeats. Obsessions and ruminations are yet another outgrowth of a disturbed and conflictual emotional state.

Concreteness

A loss of metaphorical or symbolic language is characteristic of a disturbance in thinking called *concreteness*. For example, the doctor asks the patient, "What brings you to the office today?" The usual expected response would be "I don't feel well" or "I have a pain." If the patient replies, "What brought me to the office today was a bus," then the question has been interpreted and answered concretely, and the usual metaphorical meaning of the doctor's question was lost.

Confabulation

This is a rare disturbance of thinking and involves an effort to cover up a deficit. As the word suggests, it is the telling of fictitious occurrences. It is not actually lying. In a typical example, an individual will say to a stranger: "Hello. I remember you. We met at such and such a place," when in fact there had never been such a meeting. People who confabulate believe what they are saying. They do it unconsciously and in an effort to cover their embarrassment and sense of uneasiness.

Older people are often aware of their loss of functions and become disturbed by the daily reminders that "they are not the way they should be." At the borderline between health and illness, the inability to relate to others may trigger major disturbances. Some questions that a family should openly discuss among themselves, or with a professional, concern their own reactions in terms of keeping the older person at home. Are they strong enough to tolerate deviant behaviors without harsh self-blame, guilt, or overidentification? Will their family system break down under the pressure of one of its members demanding too much careful watching? Will the disturbed person deteriorate without the continuous care that a hospital or other facility can offer?

Assessing the Risks of Disturbed Behavior

Some behaviors are deviant but in no way dangerous, whereas others present real risks. Families can be made aware of the risks involved and can be helped to determine when institutionalization is the wiser action. The following examples are given to illustrate what can be considered harmless deviant behavior and what behavior may present risks for the disturbed person.

A family sought counseling about their elderly relative who, they said, would file the soles of his shoes several times a week. There was no particular time when he would do this, but he went about the activity in a very orderly and routine way. He would place a chair in the corner of the kitchen and spread a newspaper on the floor in front of the chair. Then he would inspect each shoe very carefully for some minutes before beginning to rhythmically file away at the soles and sometimes at the heels. When he stopped filing, he would examine his shoes with pleasure and put everything away until the next time.

When the family asked him why he did this, he simply ignored their questions. Though this behavior, as well as his habit of mumbling to himself, seemed extremely bizarre, he was never anything but calm and gentle in his relationships with family and their friends. When the family was helped to deal with their feelings about the meaning of this eccentric behavior and could accept this situation, they were able to keep their relative in his home environment for the time being. Risk here was deemed to be negligible, if it existed at all, and the family acceptance definitely helped the older man.

In contrast to this benign situation is one of an aging aunt who had begun walking up to people in the street and spitting in the faces of those who, she said, "were making fun of me." The family explained that their aunt had always been very proper, almost ceremonious in her normal behavior, so that it was difficult to discuss this deviance with her. When they tried, she denied everything. Having a family member accompany her on her long walks was not helpful either. She would walk along in a seemingly relaxed mood when suddenly she would approach a stranger and make a scene.

In this case, it was suggested that the older woman needed a protective setting in which possibly both a drug regimen and psychotherapy could be enforced.

Chapter Five

Relating to the Disturbed Older Person

The applause of a single human being is of great consequence.
Samuel Johnson (from Boswell's
Life of Dr. Johnson, Vol. II, p. 291)

In Chapter Three we discussed organic disorders. In the preceding chapter we defined functional disorders. At this point, we will discuss how to deal clinically with those suffering from some form of psychological and/or neurological disorder. When speaking with older people who are generally confused, particularly about events of recent origin, one often gets the feeling that memory, confusion, disorientation, and defensive maneuvers come and go as needed. They may say things that appear to be intellectually precise, with appropriate emotional shading, and then follow these statements with remarks that are totally inappropriate. For example, a woman in a nursing home, in conversation with a therapist, said sadly, "My daughter is going to divorce her husband." And in the next instant, she chuckled and said, "I am going to have rice pudding for dessert."

Although a person may be suffering from a cognitive defect, loss of reason and loss of brain function are not always present. There are rational times when she is capable of normal communication and interaction. Communication often breaks down if the family believes that "Grandma is totally gone" and makes no effort to relate to her. This is similar to the assumption that a younger person suffering from schizophrenia (he believes that he is Napoleon or has some other grandiose idea) is to be treated as though he were deluded all the time. This is not necessarily so.

Listening Beyond What They Are Saying

An elderly woman being cared for at home by her family, despite her often confused and disoriented behavior, was interviewed by a social worker in terms of the needs of her condition. When asked how she was feeling, the woman glanced toward her husband and said, "I am good because I have a good man." The social worker agreed with her that her husband, who at eighty-nine looked after her in a most caring way, was indeed a good man. The woman added, "My husband is a good man and my son is a good man and his wife is a good man and there are good men in the forest."

Although this statement bears little resemblance to an appropriate response, a certain validity can be found in it by exploring the dynamics of this woman and her background. She was referring back to a time in her life, during the Second World War, when she and her husband lived in a forest among partisans for months at a time, hiding from the Germans. There were many "good men" among the partisans, and she remembered them and often spoke about them after her survival and emigration to the United States. What was real then seems real to her now, and perhaps some level of awareness from her past has fresh importance to her in her current life situation. Much as the good men in the forest aided her survival in years past, the good men in her family (husband, son, and daughter-in-law) are instrumental to her present survival. Once explained, her seemingly irrelevant remarks could be understood and therefore could be responded to appropriately.

Often many people prefer to avoid the bizarre or inexplicable behavior of older people because they do not know how to respond to it. Sometimes professionals, when interviewing or treating a client who exhibits "senile" symptoms, will pay attention only to those statements that seem to reflect appropriate reality testing, and will ignore everything that does not. The professional may, for example, turn away, avoid eye contact, and exclude the older person from conversation when the older person, either spontaneously, or in response to a question, makes statements that seem to be totally unrelated to the general conversation.

In ordinary circumstances, *nonreinforcement,* or not responding to bizarre behavior or statements, will encourage the person to react in a more socially appropriate manner. However, there is no evidence to indicate that nonreinforcement will help the confused older person. In fact, clinical observations indicate that often the opposite occurs. When older people, who are the focal point of the discussion, are not being included, they seem to become more depressed and withdrawn, more "out of it." They may look down at the floor, mutter to themselves, or look into the distance. Lack of attention at this time seems to exacerbate their anxiety, and they respond with random, inappropriate behavior.

One-Sided Conversations

Grappling with the mixed emotions of their own guilt, anger, bewilderment, disappointment, and their desire to help, family members are often unable to express genuine concern for a disoriented parent. Often conversational exchanges between child and parent at a time of crisis approximate a courtroom drama, with the visiting child assuming the role of prosecuting attorney in the cross-examination of an unfriendly witness. "Did the doctor come to see you today?" "Did he change your medication?" "What did he say?" "When is he coming again?" "Did you tell him about your pain, your fall, your lapse of memory?" As anxiety mounts at the lack of normal conversational give-and-take, the visiting child may feel more comfortable and in control when asking the parent specific questions. When responses falter and silences grow longer, the child is then at a loss as to what to say or do in the frightening situation of trying to communicate with a person who is only appropriately responsive some of the time. Confrontation methods serve no purpose with confused older people. A demanding approach only intensifies their confusion, as their losses cannot be restored. Therefore, if one can become aware of the processes of decline and adjust to them, some acceptance of the changes in behavior may possibly be made.

Understanding Your Own Feelings

Watching a loved one decline into dependency is frightening. Communicating with older people who are confused is painful and difficult. What does one say to people who used to make a lot of sense and are no longer coherent, who are confused about the time of day and their time of life, and who sometimes do not even recognize their own children? It is human nature, and good adaptive behavior, to avoid what hurts.

Grown children, living away from their mother, visit her, but they don't say much to her. "She keeps repeating things anyway. Yesterday she cried again, because her father died." Daughter says: "Mama, he's been dead for twenty-two years." The mother did not seem to hear, but goes on talking about her father's death as if it happened yesterday. Her children stop correcting her. Soon they stop visiting her. Then they look for excuses not to feel guilty. It is easy to find excuses. They tell themselves that they have no time. Their visits may even upset her; the adult residence or nursing home staff never seems all that pleased to see visitors; their mother seems to be getting good care without them. But most of all, they rationalize, she does not recognize her children when they visit. In this way they ease their guilt, their shame, and their possible overidentification with their parent. The vast majority of children/caregivers are at the end of their middle years, approaching retirement age themselves. Their fears and pain are real, not the least of which is the worry, "Will I be like that when I am that age?"

Yet, as we know, studies show that there is little truth to the myth that American children are uncaring about their aging parents. Much evidence indicates that they care, even those who do not live near their parents. Our highly mobile way of life has split up many families, but at the same time people use all the devices available to them in this industrialized society to show that they care. They create intimacy at a distance with the telephone, and they send telegrams and letters. They use airplanes, trains, buses, and cars. They visit, but they also avoid when they don't know what to do.

"What do I do when she doesn't know who I am?"

"What do I do when she mistakes me for my sister, who died thirty years ago?"

"What do I say when Papa just talks gibberish?"

"Every time I visit, she tells me, 'I don't want to see anyone.' Then two minutes later she complains that no one comes to see her."

Although the problems of communication may be great, it is most important to find ways to deal with the aged person's anxiety and frustration, while also paying attention to our own feelings. Nearly all older people, except those who are totally disoriented, respond according to the way they are treated and spoken to. We all do, for that matter. The following script or scenario suggests a general method of approach to conversation and contact with an older person who has memory and behavioral problems.

A Scenario

The more contact you make, the more relaxed you will feel. The older person (we'll call her Mother) may be up and about, or she may often be sitting in a chair. Occasionally she may be lying in bed. However she may be when you visit, you should try to get to the same level, face to face. Sit or position yourself so that you are directly in front of her or within an easy range of view.

What helps the most is staying *real* for Mother. When she says that today is Tuesday and it is, in fact, Sunday, don't agree with her. This will only add to the disorientation from which she is already suffering. Instead, provide a flow of reality. Repeat, repeat, repeat what she needs to know. Tell her over and over *where* she is; what the *date* is; what the *time* is; *who* you are; *what* is happening; and tell her the *next thing* to do. Say it clearly, loudly, and slowly. Give her plenty of time to answer. Older people may not hear as well as the young. They also don't like to think of themselves as being incompetent and may not ask you to repeat even when they have failed to hear or to understand you. Be aware of the declines and complement them.

Talk to Mother in a normal conversational tone, even though you are saying the same thing over and over. Don't talk down to her, as though she is a recalcitrant child. Correct her when she makes erroneous statements and reinforce her each time she makes an appropriate remark. You reinforce in the simple ways we use each day with all people: You smile, you nod your head; you look into her eyes acceptingly; you say "That's right," "That's fine," or "That's good."

Staying real shows your acceptance of Mother. It reflects a caring attitude. Ignoring her incorrect statements, or going along with them, or appeasing her, or cajoling her inevitably leads to feelings of anxiety and depression and to even more bizarre behavior on her part. Acceptance can lead to feelings of increased security, self-worth, and self-esteem, which may help give her a purpose, a will to go on. At least it provides stimulation in an environment that may be woefully lacking in it.

A sensitive listener can understand more than the words a person is saying. There are intonations, facial expressions, and body language. With a confused older person, one can learn to "read" certain subtle cues in body movement; one can also learn to decode or interpret garbled statements. Obviously, it will go slowly at first, so patience and motivation are needed, for habits of a lifetime may be difficult to overcome or to compensate for in some parent-child relationships.

To respond to Mother's verbal or behavioral peculiarities by becoming angry, argumentative, or by feeling hurt is natural enough, but does not help at all. Instead, it is more helpful to become aware of what you are feeling, to accept it, and to try to understand it. For example, if you feel hurt at not being recognized by Mother, it may be because you believe that if she really always loved you and knew you in the way you wished, this nonrecognition would not have come about. Yet you may also know this is not true and that Mother can't help her condition, which has little to do with you. Being aware of both sides of the picture, the reality and your response, will help you to deal with the situation without neglect to either your parent or yourself.

Reality Orientation as a Helpful Approach

Be patient and listen. Helping her relate to herself in terms of time, place, and persons is known therapeutically as *reality orientation*. For example, when she thinks it is Sunday and you explain to her, "No, today is Tuesday," you can also say, "I know it may seem like Sunday to you because I am here now and I sometimes visit on Sundays. But today is Tuesday and I am visiting you today."

You may notice her clutching a blanket or doll, holding it to her and calling it "my baby." It is not necessary to take away the object. But it helps to say, "Mama, that is a doll you are holding. It must be very important to you." Let her keep it, but let her know that it is a doll—not a baby. Bring her back to reality gently, and show her you understand some of her feelings. Don't just think it, say it. It can be effective. It is not an easy thing to do, to communicate with her in this way. To see a parent in this condition, remembering what she was once like, is painful. Yet even now, it may be that she is not always disoriented. Sometimes she does know the day, the time, when she was born, and when you were born. And, of course, you can't help thinking that she once knew all this, and much more.

Love and Hate Can Go Together

Feeling and expressing emotion is real, and means we are alive. We have all kinds of emotions: love, hate, joy, anxiety, ecstasy, guilt, fear, despair. The forces of religion, history, culture, and collective experience in our heritage have made many of us believe that there are "good" emotions and "bad" ones. We frown on the "bad" emotions, such as hate and anger; we praise the "good" ones, such as love and joy. This attitude can produce intolerable tensions. There are positive sides to anger and anxiety. For example, without anxiety, you would not know that you are in danger. It acts as an alarm by alerting you to possible dangers in a potentially harmful situation. An inner antenna goes up and sounds a warning; in this way, anxiety can be protective. If someone were walking too closely behind you on a dark city street, anxiety would make you sense the presence and act in a way to defend yourself. Anger can prepare us for action by telling us when something we do not like is happening. These signals tell us that we are alive and open to a range of many different emotions, each suited to particular situations. "Bad" emotions are as natural and normal as "good" ones. All emotions are normal. The critical factor is being aware of what we are experiencing, for then we control our emotions rather than letting them control us.

The older person may express anger, too. She may resent what life has done to her. People may be treating her with indifference. She may resent her impaired physical, mental, and emotional condition; her lack of control over her environment; and all the losses she has suffered in her later life. Wishing her to be quiet, passive, serene, and uncomplaining is to deny her a life-force. Stripping her of emotions, both the "good" and "bad," is stripping her of the will to live and fight back. This can lead to depression, to apathy, and to a final giving up.

Don't be afraid of emotions—they signify life. Understand them, accept them, deal with them. Then make choices about what to do with them. Remember that love and hate can go together. So can happiness and sorrow, envy and gratitude. We can tolerate contradictory feelings and yet remain the same person, so that we can both love and hate another person. This kind of ambivalent feeling starts when we are very little, loving our parents even when they have denied us something that we very much wanted. Frustration led to anger and rage at them. Still, we loved them. Now, many years later, we should recognize that our parents are entitled to the same privilege. They have the same privilege. They have the same emotional range. They can also show frustration and anger and still love us. If we can accept conflicting emotions in ourselves, we can accept them in others, including our parents in their later years or, indeed, at any time. If we are not afraid of our own emotions, we will not be afraid of theirs. Mutual acceptance can provide a bond. And a bond with another person is the optimum to be wished for everyone, however "disturbed" she appears to be.

Chapter Six

Nursing Home Placement and Family Decisions

It cannot be too often repeated that the growing old of the body does not mean that the spirit has to grow old too.

(Ashley Montague, *Growing Young*)

At some time in the life of most families a decision must be made about the future health care of an elderly relative who is seriously ill and physically incapacitated. This decision is usually made in accord with a physician's suggestion that the patient be transferred to an environment that provides full-time supervision in carrying out the activities of daily living (ADL) such as eating, dressing, bathing, as well as providing physical and recreational therapy and supervising of medication. The impetus for this decision may arise because a daughter, who has been the main provider of care for a chronically sick mother, can no longer continue alone, and asks her siblings for help. Or a widowed parent is suddenly stricken and no longer able to live alone, and the children must decide "what to do about Mother." It is always extremely difficult, even among the most cohesive families, when the prospect of institutionalization for a loved one must be considered.

Family Roles in Decision Making

Crisis brings the family together once again to act in unity. Although they have probably lived apart for many years, quickly and subtly they begin to reenact their former roles with one another. "Big brother" bends protectively in his traditional benign role to his "little sis," the "baby" of the family. The "good one" is compliant, while the "dictator" seems ready to tell everyone what to do. Past roles and sometimes past resentments are rekindled. Stress is felt by everyone, for not only do brothers and sisters have to contend with one another, but wives' and husbands' opinions must also be considered. Often the family replays various scenes from its past in order to act together in the present.

Although they meet with a common concern, to find the best solution for the remaining years of their parents's life, feelings may range from deep attachment to cool detachment for this parent. Each child is born at a particular time in the history of the family and shaped by many events beyond his or her control. Though no longer young, they may still be coping with familiar syndromes: of the first born, the middle child, the "favored child" or the "problem child." The formative years of one child may have occurred during a secure period in the life of the family, whereas the other children may have known sadness or separation as a result of divorce or the death of a parent. One child seemed to get all the parents' attention, yet she may still feel that the others had more love and affection. Many old ties as well as unresolved conflicts must be addressed when the family is drawn together for this common purpose.

Cooperation and Compromise: A Case Example

A case in point is a family we will call the Sandlers. As a result of a severely disabling stroke, the mother, Denise Sandler, is partially paralyzed. She is ready to leave the hospital but is not able to go back to living on her own, nor can any of her three children take her into their home. Her physician recommends nursing home placement. Lloyd, her eldest child, agrees without hesitation. "None of us is able to give Mother the care she needs, so there is nothing else to do but find a good place where she will be well looked after," he tells them.

Despite the need for quick action, his brother and sister anguish over the decision and deliberate while he grows impatient with them. This has been the pattern of their lives together. Lloyd is the decisive one who has always made the major decisions in the family. His parents were very young when he was born and then waited ten years before having another child, a son named Ira. Two years later, their daughter, Nancy, was born. They seemed to be more relaxed and able to relate better, with more warmth and affection, to the younger children than they did to Lloyd, who, even as a little boy, was considered independent and self-motivated. New parents often make demands on their oldest child, pushing him or her to be super-independent, either out of inexperience in parenting or out of their unconscious need for parenting themselves. Thus, a new family developed in which the younger children viewed Lloyd as part of the parental system, a role he fully accepted. Although he always made himself available when they needed him for financial help or for advice, he was emotionally distant from his parents and siblings, while they maintained very close ties with one another.

Nancy and Ira had no solution to the problem of their mother's care, yet agonized over the decision, relying upon Lloyd as always to convince them that this was the only thing to do. When they were finally persuaded, Ira and Nancy took full responsibility for finding a suitable nursing home for their mother.

This task, of seeking geriatric care for parents no longer capable of managing alone, produces much anxiety among the children, who are usually in their middle years or older. Fear that this may happen to them is sometimes so overwhelming that it interferes with the love and respect they have for the parent. They may unconsciously and sometimes consciously resent a mother's abdication of parental care and feel imprisoned by her dependence on them. While trying to do everything they can to help her, they nonetheless feel guilty, powerless, and apprehensive when releasing her to the care of strangers.

The reasons for these feelings are complex and deeply rooted. A daughter may need to believe that she is always in total control, so much so that she is unable to allay her sense of omnipotence that makes her feel she should be able to know everything, do everything, and have total control in all situations, even of someone's illness and of death itself. All she can think is, "If only I can find the right doctor or nurse and make Mother well again. If anything goes wrong in the nursing home, it will be my fault."

A son may feel he has abandoned his parent at a time of great need, when that need is finite. "Dad may live only a short time longer, yet I simply cannot keep him at home anymore," he anguishes. There is no way to predict how long his father will live, whether it be a few weeks or a few years, but if the burden of care has for some time been almost beyond endurance, then a realistic assessment needs to be made. Certain questions should be asked: What effect does the father's constant care have on the son's mental and physical well-being? On his family's? On his financial resources? If the son can admit to having done the best he could, and that continuing as caregiver to his father, who is growing progressively worse, will undermine his own health and his family's well-being, then realistically he should seek nursing home placement for his parent and not burden himself with guilt for coming to this decision.

The Burden of Guilt

Feelings of guilt are not easy to control. They relate to unresolved conflicts from the past. For instance, a boy may have wished that no siblings be born, wished for his father to go away, perhaps even to die, and then feared punishment for having such unacceptable impulses. When intense feelings remain unresolved throughout a lifetime, they may reemerge in times of crisis, covered over by much rational talk.

Guilt is triggered by unconscious motivations surrounded by societal attitudes. We are taught to take individual responsibility for everything we do and for what we think we should do. We are taught to overcome human weakness in ourselves; we feel morally responsible when we fail. Society's messages are clear and strong: "Stand on your own two feet." "Keep a stiff upper lip." "You are responsible for your failures." These messages make it difficult for both the dependent elderly to ask for help and for the care-giver, usually a woman, to relinquish her role when the burden becomes too great. Because she was raised to believe that she is meant to mother and nurture, to live for others and through others, the care-giver often overlooks her own needs. Yet when people cling to precepts they think they should unquestioningly adhere to while going beyond the limits of their endurance, they may destroy the essence of the family life they strive to uphold. The quality of their relationships may be impaired by bitterness, resentment, and despair as they begin to wonder about all the good years they had together—or indeed, if there were any good years at all. At this crossroad in a family's life, it may be more beneficial for everyone concerned to seek nursing home placement for the ailing older person who, no longer vital or capable, is in need of constant care and attention.

Including the Older Person in Decision Making

While tensions may ease somewhat as the family begins to consider alternative solutions, the future may seem terrifying for the older person waiting in uncertainty while others decide her fate. The more the patient is involved in the discussion and planning, the less shocked and helpless she will feel at the time of transfer. Even an older person who seems confused and incoherent has times of lucidity and should be included in the discussions when at all possible.

Looking for a Suitable Facility

Once the family has come to terms with their decision, the next task is to find a suitable health care facility. This task may seem overwhelming at first. How does one begin? Where are nursing homes located? Which are the best ones? Are family members allowed to visit them before making a choice? How do they make an appointment for a tour? How much do these facilities cost? Will the family qualify for financial assistance?

Preliminary information may be obtained from the patient's physician, the local medical society, social service agencies, community welfare offices, Social Security office, and the state chapters of the American Health Care Association (for proprietary, or private, homes) and the American Association of Homes for the Aging (for nonprofit homes).

Institutional Levels of Care

The quality of care and the surroundings vary considerably among health care facilities, as they do in every kind of service industry. In the mid-1960s, Medicaid and Medicare programs gave impetus to the building boom in nursing homes, which developed into a multibillion-dollar industry. More than 75 percent of the approximately nineteen thousand long-term health care facilities for the aged are privately owned and operated for profit. In the mid-1960s there seemed to be valid reasons for this development: the increasing number of frail elderly; the decline of the extended family; and the belief that moving stabilized elderly patients out of hospitals and into less expensive nursing facilities would reduce the costs of hospitalization. This last point soon proved to be incorrect, because the money saved from shorter hospital stays was offset by the larger costs of long-term institutionalization. Consequently, long-term-care facilities were divided into three classes to correspond to different levels and costs of treatment.

There are skilled nursing facilities (SNFs); intermediate care facilities (ICFs); and domiciliary care, or board and care homes for adults (DCFs). These are meant to correspond to the patient's needs for nursing and other services, so that a patient with severe impairment would enter an SNF; the moderately impaired, an ICF; and the mildly impaired, a DCF. However, recent research (Holmes et al., 1982) indicates that while there is a considerable difference in degrees of impairment between individuals in skilled nursing facilities (SNFs) and the other two levels, the differences in residents' impairment is not so great between the intermediate and the residential facilities.

Skilled nursing facilities and intermediate care facilities are both federally regulated. They receive a subsidy for patients from Social Security (Medicaid and Medicare), whereas residential homes for adults are not federally regulated, and conditions in these vary from state to state.

A skilled nursing facility (SNF) is intended for people who require continual nursing supervision and must have a registered nurse on duty at all times. Larger SNFs (those with more than sixty patients) must have at least two registered nurses on duty as charge nurses at all times; and they must also have a medical director. An intermediate care facility (ICF), while subject to all the federal safety restrictions and environmental codes, has less stringent rules regarding medical supervision. There is no specification for the number of nurses required per patient, but a nurse must be available to dispense medications. To be admitted to either a skilled nursing facility or an intermediate care facility and still be eligible for Medicare and Medicaid coverage, a physician must recommend placement and certify that the patient needs care. The patient may then be subjected to utilization review by a committee appointed by the institution.

Board and Care, or residential homes (DCFs), are generally for people who need some help in dressing, cooking, shopping, eating, bathing, or other activities of daily living (ADL), but who do not have an illness requiring special medical care and twenty-four-hour nursing. Few environmental restraints (number of beds in a room, proximity of toilets, fire regulations, safety precautions) are imposed by federal or state regulation. Rules regarding nursing availability vary from state to state. It is estimated that there are about thirty thousand of these facilities, which range in size from small adult homes where the owner lives on the premises and cares for two or three elderly individuals, to large settings with over two hundred beds. Board and Care facilities are different from boarding homes which provide room and board only, without services.

The Nursing Home Population

The majority of the population in skilled nursing facilities (SNFs) is over the age of seventy-five. About three quarters are women; about half do not have family living nearby, if they have any close family at all. Many nursing home residents have outlived their spouse and sometimes even their children. Only about 12 percent are married. At least half suffer from senile dementia. Many are incontinent of bladder and bowel. Most become progressively worse and die within two and a half years of entering. It is said that nursing homes provide only warehousing or cold storage, but for the majority of sick elderly who reside in them, this is often the only place they have to live out their remaining years. The stigma attached to nursing homes is in part due to past history and in part to more recent scandals. In the early nineteenth century, the indigent poor of all ages and the mentally incompetent were taken to almshouses, which to a great extent were considered cruel and inhuman institutions in their time, when general living conditions were far more severe than they are today. This negative image was reinforced in the late 1960s and early 1970s, when investigations found deplorable conditions in many proprietary nursing homes run by unscrupulous speculators. As a result, the government placed more regulations on nursing home owners, but still there remains a very wide range of care, from those that provide very proficient and humane care to homes where patients are poorly fed and treated, overly sedated and left to languish in bed or in front of a fixed-channel television set. It is difficult, if not impossible, for patients in nursing homes to act as informed consumers. It is therefore up to kin and friends and the government to be watchful and to protect them from abuse.

The nursing home experience need not be negative if a facility that can best meet the patient's needs is selected. It can then be an acceptable solution to the problems of providing essential physical and medical care, fulfilling basic daily needs, and offering security and protection, particularly for the confused and frail patient.

A first visit to a skilled nursing facility may be very distressing to people who have never been to one before. A not uncommon reaction to a first visit is "I couldn't wait to get out of there!" However, it is necessary to visit several facilities and sometimes to go back to those initially rejected in order to make comparisons for a selective decision. It helps everyone involved when a few family members are willing to share the responsibility. For instance, the person who is best at coping with details and understanding the small print on contracts could be responsible for dealing with bureaucratic procedures relating to Social Security benefits, tax credits, personal exemptions, and so forth.

Using the Sandler family as a model, it was Lloyd who handled these aspects, while Ira and Nancy inspected the facilities, questioned the personnel, and discussed their impressions with one another. Since Nancy would be the most frequent, regular visitor, they decided to look for a facility close to her home.

It is necessary to make appointments in advance to tour prospective health care facilities, and it is useful to bring a checklist because, under emotional strain, it is easy to forget many of the questions you intend to ask.

Staff-Patient Relationships

There is much you can learn about a place just by observing how the staff treat the patients. Do the staff appear to be kind and address the patients with respect, or are they patronizing and impatient with them? Are the residents dressed in nightclothes or in street clothes? Ask if you may visit at mealtime, so you can see what the food looks like and how the patients look when they are eating. Do they seem overly sedated?

You will be shown the living arrangements. Notice whether the rooms are spacious, how close together the beds are placed, if dresser drawers open and shut easily, if there are handrails in the corridors and grab bars in the bathrooms. Ask to see the facilities for bathing and observe if there are showers or tubs in the bathrooms.

There are many questions to ask. Are patients given physiotherapy and recreation therapy on a regular basis? Are they allowed to have some of their possessions in their rooms? Notice whether or not the bedrooms have patients' personal touches. You will want to know about the staff-patient ratio and the qualifications of the staff. Are aides trained by the facility or have they been trained prior to employment? (The latter is preferable.) Does staff include physicians, registered nurses, dieticians, social workers? Who is on duty at night? Find out who is in charge. It is not a good sign if the administrator is seldom available. Absentee management sets a poor precedent for staff and may lead to an atmosphere of indifference and neglect. The quality of care—in terms of friendliness and warmth, flexibility yet adherence to routine, and the degree of personal dignity with which patients are treated—emanates mostly from the attitude and expectations of the administration. These and other pointers are given by Silverstone and Hyman in *You and Your Aging Parent* (1976, pp. 202-220).

The Transition from Home to Nursing Home

For older people who have lived their long lives in extended families, the transition from private residence to nursing home residence is likely to be overwhelming at first, no matter how efficiently the institution provides them with the care they need. Consider what distresses you during your short visits and try to imagine what it must be like to spend your days surrounded by people who for the most part sit apathetically, move slowly in wheelchairs and walkers, sometimes talk to themselves or suddenly cry out in anguish when nobody answers. Nursing home residents do not communicate very much with one another. Those who are mentally alert feel that they do not belong where they are. In avoiding the less competent patients (who are in the majority), they also feel isolated. Their losses must seem overwhelming as they no longer fulfill their old roles of breadwinner, housekeeper, friend, wife, and parent. When entering a nursing home, they are usually compelled to relinquish the possessions of a lifetime, to pare down their belongings to items that will fit into a clothes closet and one or two chests of drawers. No longer responsible for their money, they have small amounts doled out to them weekly. They have lost their privacy, individuality, and independence. They may no longer come and go freely, nor do they have the choice of what to eat and when. Most decisions are made for them, not by them.

Although most of us live our lives according to fixed schedules (for work, for meals, for bedtime, and for recreation), and accept this, there is a world of difference between a normal daily routine and that of a patient in an institutional setting where activities must be routinized if they are to function efficiently in providing the care needed by severely impaired persons and at the same time be cost-effective.

Some people will recognize the aspects of their dependencies and avail themselves of the help at hand without fear or shame, yet still take responsibility wherever they can. Others will become increasingly dependent and passively accept their lot with little or no resistance, while there are those who will shrink from life and decline rapidly. The initial period of adjustment will be difficult not only for the patient, but also for the family, who will feel vulnerable and uncertain in an unfamiliar environment.

In some facilities, when aides are available and ready to help, staff ask relatives to spend as much time there as possible in the early days after admission. In other facilities, staff prefer family to stay in the background until the new patient has become somewhat used to the rules, the routines, and the people. The more families learn about the method and regulations *in advance*, the more easily they will adapt to the new setting and find an appropriate role within its complex organizational structure. At the same time, they can deal with their feelings of ambivalence at having placed their kin in an institution.

The Family as a Link Between Patient and Staff

In some families, habitual roles may change as the members adapt to the new situation. For instance, once Denise Sandler was transferred from the hospital to a nursing home, it was Nancy, not Lloyd, who assumed the responsibility for seeing that appropriate treatment was given by the staff. Since Lloyd's manner was somewhat overbearing, his sister suggested that he take a less dominant role. Used to issuing orders, he would tell the staff in no uncertain terms that he expected his mother's requests to be answered immediately. He wished others to respond to his mother as they would to him. In no time at all, he antagonized most staff members and made his mother feel uneasy during his visits because he wished her to be demanding and assertive, maintaining that if she were not, she would be neglected.

Nancy, visiting often and with regularity, became the link between her mother and staff. She dealt with minor complaints about food, the need for a new dress, the problems about lost clothing, broken eyeglasses, or a faulty hearing aid. She discussed her mother's medical condition with the staff and knew who provided help with medication, with dressing and bathing, and with physiotherapy. Because she was confined to a wheelchair, Denise Sandler needed constant assistance in exercising, since the more she exercised, the better she felt. Nancy helped her when she visited, yet knew her mother's schedule and did not come at those times when staff would be occupied with her treatment.

Coping Strategies for Patient and Family

The patient (and the family) uses adaptive strategies to fit into the new environment. People who are used to living alone or who have spent their lives within the family may find it difficult to adjust to communal living, but untapped coping skills can emerge.

Since all people are different, at all ages, their responses will vary. For some the nursing home environment may provide too much stimulation, while for others it does not provide enough. One patient may prefer more privacy than is available, but adaptively finds ways to obtain time alone. Paradoxically, the person who demands attention by shouting and displaying abusive behavior often does, in fact, receive more attention than unassuming, compliant patients like Denise Sandler. A person who can no longer delay gratification may find it difficult to live in a setting where long delays need to be tolerated. For these reasons, children may sometimes have to act as mediators between patient and staff. If the family finds that their complaints do not help and that the situation continues to be intolerable, it may be necessary to find another facility. A nursing home should provide residents with the opportunity to function at an optimum level despite major physical and mental deficits. Everyone adjusts individually to all situations, including new, unfamiliar ones.

Complaining Is a Form of Communicating

Thus, while some people appear to complain all the time, driving everyone into a frenzy, it may be their only way of communicating. Even under ideal conditions, they will find much to criticize. It is their wish for perfection. In the less-than-perfect world of nursing homes, where major daily activities are conducted in group settings by overworked staff, one can expect that the most stoic of individuals will, at times, express displeasure. For example, complaints about food are very common in institutional environments. To accommodate the large number of diets that are restrictive, cooking is salt-free and sugar-free, and sometimes not too tasty. Patients may complain that everything they eat tastes bitter. This may be because medication affects their sense of taste. Despite the reality of the complaints, what can be considered is that food is a primary way in which we are sustained; it was the first source of gratification to us as infants. As such, it has tremendous meaning, both actual and symbolic. It is a way of being given to, a form of receiving care and nurturance. A woman can complain about the food and really mean that the environment, the staff, her son, or a visiting relative is not satisfying a basic need. Unaware of this, and knowing that complaining about food is an acceptable means of expression, she may talk incessantly about the overcooked meat or vegetables. It is easier talking about unpalatable food than "unpalatable" people! One way to determine what is going on is to check the food yourself. Have a meal with your parent or relative to determine if the medication is affecting her taste buds. If this is not the case, check her diet and any restrictions she is subject to. Most importantly, think of what it is that she may be really complaining about. Frequent visits are necessary in order to make a realistic assessment of the situation and the need for effecting change.

Visiting Your Relative

Visits can be difficult. A mother may not recognize her daughter, or not remember that she had just visited the day before, while the daughter, caught in anxiety, wonders if she needs to go at all. The parent, in adapting to new demands, may become dependent upon the institutional staff and the new friends she has made. These may exert a stronger influence than news of family life told during conversations with visiting children. Therefore, visits need to be thought through in terms of what they now communicate to both parent and child. Past expectations may need to be modified and the normal conversational give-and-take of the past may no longer be possible. Sometimes a visit may mean just sitting close and holding the hand of a severely impaired person who may not seem to be aware of whose hand she is holding. These visits can be less painful if they are anticipated. Bringing tape recordings of music familiar to the patient or materials for handicrafts, or playing favorite games or looking through family photo albums and reminiscing are ways of bringing pleasure into visits.

Frequency of contact and the way the family responds to the patient in a nursing home may determine staff care and responsiveness. Staff are apt to give more attention to patients of concerned families with whom they can discuss the patient's needs than with a family who appears uninvolved or with a family who, after placing a parent in a nursing home, departs as soon as she is installed, never or seldom to be seen again.

Relocation Can Be Stressful

While the majority of older people in a crisis situation remain in the facility that was available at the time of need, about 30 percent of patients leave skilled nursing facilities to return to their home or to residential care facilities. Whereas rehabilitation and discharge should be the top priority for those institutionalized, oddly, successful treatment sometimes creates other problems. For example, a woman who was bedridden because of acute dizziness and severe back pain went to a nursing home because she needed help with feeding, dressing, and washing. Though continent, she was not able to get up and go to the toilet by herself. Gradually, with trained care, she became stronger, able to wash her hands and face, and then to dress herself. She was encouraged to walk, despite her fear of falling. With daily training, she grew physically stronger and eventually developed confidence enough to allow her to be moved from a skilled nursing facility to an intermediate-level care facility (ICF). However, as soon as she learned that she was to be transferred, her condition deteriorated and she became bedridden again. She wished to stay where she was. This event is not at all uncommon. The woman in our example had adjusted to the new place, where she was treated well. She had made new friends. Understandably, she did not want to leave the familiar surroundings for strange ones. For a healthy person, change can be stressful, if also challenging, whether the move is to a new neighborhood, a new school, or a new job. For a physically dependent older person to contemplate yet another move to an unknown place can be extremely upsetting.

Families as well can become upset when they must either find another suitable facility or make a place in their home once again. Often, when the responsibility of care has been removed, they are reluctant to reassume it. To assure a minimum of unnecessary change, it is helpful when choosing a facility initially to consider one that contains within its premises different levels of care such as a skilled nursing facility and also an intermediate nursing facility, thus enabling transfer when needed with a minimum of change.

New Responses to Old Problems

Sometimes a crisis may actually strengthen family ties. The ability to respond to new situations can emerge as positive feelings, even when there have been lifelong difficulties.

For instance, a widow had for several years lived for varying amounts of time with each of her three children. This had been a family decision taken before their father had died. "We'll never send Mom to one of those places," they assured him. Yet each child was relieved when she moved on to a sibling's home for a few months. As they grew older themselves, they had their own problems with retirement, finances, and illness, and they became more and more upset by their mother's increasing dependence. This family had never been close and saw each other more out of a sense of duty to their parents than because they wanted to be together. They found it hard to be candid with one another until their conflicts and guilt began to peak, as each wondered "what to do about Mother."

Finally they agreed, for the good of all concerned, including that of their mother, that she should go to a retirement home. They sought counseling to persuade her to agree to go. She was less able to get around on her own, and although she lived with their families, she felt quite isolated, but would not admit it. Also, she sensed that they felt burdened with caring for her; once all this was openly discussed, she came to terms with the fact that all would benefit were she to move to a residential setting. Together with her children, she went to find a suitable facility.

Soon after she went into residential care, her children began to relate to her as they had not done since before she was widowed. They seemed to see a new woman, one they admired because of the way she adapted to her new situation. She made friends with people who were alert, as she was, and was liked and respected by the staff. During visits, conversation was more interesting and animated than it had been all the time they lived together. She told her children what she liked and what she did not like about institutional living, and how she had to firmly set boundaries for herself so residents she did not want to be with would not encroach upon her. Thus, they understood her complaints and did what they could to make life easier for her.

She had not suddenly become a "new woman" at the age of eighty-five. Those qualities that made it possible for her to adjust to a new environment had always been there, but she had not been given the opportunity to call upon them because of the restrictive way in which she lived, as a perennial guest to reluctant hosts. Under these conditions, the change provided relief for the entire family. The children became more supportive of her and of one another, and all felt better for it. The mother's self-esteem improved as well, and living in a protected environment gave her a greater sense of security than she had felt when she spent so much time alone as an unwanted guest in her children's homes.

Chapter Seven

Critical Periods in the Family

*To everything there is a season,
And a time to every purpose under the heaven:
A time to be born, and a time to die;
A time to plant, and a time to pluck up that
which is planted . . . .*

Ecclesiastes

A family's pattern of behavior begins as a husband and wife integrate their fantasies of marriage with the realities of their relationship. All relationships—those between lovers as well as those between parents and children—are entered into with anticipation and with anxiety about the promise of fulfillment. Everyone has unspoken wishes, and needs to feel that their world is safe and good; but throughout their lives, some people assign the task of making their dreams become reality to other people, and do not realize that they are demanding omnipotence or perfection of their parents and later of their spouse.

Sustaining a stable family life requires a considerable degree of awareness, because relationships constantly alter. The youngest generation is growing up, reaching for independence, becoming brash and self-assertive, while the oldest generation is moving slowly in another direction.

When Family Roles Change

Feelings about change in older people are frequently negative or ambivalent. At fifty, many people look to the changing aspects of their middle years with increasing concern and self-absorption. They listen to their biological clock ticking away while viewing the decreasing energies and power of their parents. A widowed mother goes to live with a daughter who does not want to be the base of her needs. The mother goes to a retirement home, where she may develop a whole new extended family and a new perspective. Nevertheless, the day she leaves her daughter's home, she feels intense grief.

At this stage of a parent-child relationship, there is often the fear of irreconcilable change, based on the concept of role reversal, when it is believed the daughter expects to become "mother to the mother." This is one of the most pejorative myths of *ageism*. Despite becoming frail and lacking certain controls, and no matter what amount of care is needed, the older person is not regressing back to an earlier, childlike state. Assuming this is to deny lifetime change. Rather, this person, even if ashamed and humiliated at needing extensive care, remains a parent by virtue of years of shared experiences and a long-lasting interpersonal relationship with the child. Whatever care is provided—whether it is total care, supervision, or financial assistance—this help, when given by an adult child to an elderly parent, is not an indication of role reversal. In actuality, their relationship always remains that of child to parent, even when behaviors now seem to show increased attention by the child for the parent. More likely, the reversal in roles relates to the shift in *power* relationships which accompanies growth and change in the family. Sometimes, though, the stresses resulting from parental dependence are related to long-standing and unresolved family interactions.

*Longtime Conflicts:
Mother-Daughter Interaction*

For example, a woman sought counseling, ostensibly for her mother, in order to deal with the "problem" of the eighty-two-year-old woman's insistence on living on her own. The mother was at the time widowed for just over ten years. After her husband's death, she decided to stay in their home, which was in an apartment building in a deteriorating, high-crime neighborhood. Her sons and her only daughter expressed great concerns for her safety. "We wish that Mother would be reasonable and move to a residential hotel for the aged so we wouldn't have to worry about her all the time. But mother is stubborn and always has been. She is also hard of hearing, but won't get a hearing aid. I call her every day, but if she isn't near the telephone, she doesn't hear it, so then I have to rush over to make sure she's all right. I ask her to call me, but she does so only when she wants something." Pausing to control her tears, the daughter continued, "She complains that I don't talk to her, yet when we visit she never has anything to say to me. She talks to my husband all the time, about her savings and Social Security. He's an accountant. I could stay home for all she ever notices me. In bad weather I shop for her, and even then, she must have it her way. She expects me to shop in her neighborhood because it's cheaper than mine.

"Recently I had my sixtieth birthday and my husband made a party for me. Everyone came. My children and grandchildren, my brothers and their wives, and, of course, Mother came. They all brought presents, not that I need anything, it's just the thought. Even my little grandchildren had something for me, beautiful drawings they made in nursery school. Not my mother. As usual, she came empty-handed. She never gave me a present when I was a child, so I guess I am a fool to expect anything now," she said. "We want her to get someone to stay with her, yet she won't hear of it. We want her to get an extension phone, so she will hear us when we call, but she won't do that. I am going out of my mind with worry about her and she doesn't even notice!"

The daughter's anger and anguish over past hurts are deep and real, yet she is still hopeful that her mother will change her ways and become the reasonable person she wants her to be. And that she will also finally give to her all the love, attention, and recognition she has always needed but never received from her.

If mother and daughter could talk candidly to one another, perhaps they could state their disappointments and wishes, but never allowing this intimacy before, the women stay embedded in a rigid relationship that allows little room for growth or change. The daughter continues to seek the love and acknowledgment she resentfully feels she never had from her mother; and the mother pursues her familiar routine.

In exploring the mother's past, it was learned that she was raised in Eastern Europe, in poverty and in fear of persecution for her religious beliefs. At a young age she married a man who became a gambler. Throughout their marriage there were times when they had quite a lot of money, but many other times when he gave her nothing with which to pay the grocer. She learned to skimp and save, to do with very little, to want very little, even in good times, and she gave very little.

Her style, when under stress, was to tighten and shrink into herself. Having lived often under precarious conditions, she was always ready to withdraw and turn a cold shoulder to any potential source of rejection. It was easier to remain aloof than to engage and be hurt. After eighty-two years of practice, it was the only way she understood, and since she felt no anxiety and was in control, had no reason to consider change.

The daughter asked her mother to see a counselor, in the hope that she would be persuaded to leave her deteriorating apartment for a better place to live, but the mother refused, so the daughter went alone. In discussing her mother's problems and how unyielding the older woman was, she began to see that her own typical responses were also deeply grooved. In trying to get her mother's attention and affection, she began to see how she went out of her way to act caring and benign, to offer herself as deserving of recognition. When she began to understand her role in their relationship, she became motivated to learn more about herself; she began to feel more in charge of her life. Ideally, change should be within the family system, in that both mother and daughter will find a mutually satisfying resolution to their problem or problems with one another. However, when this is not possible, there may be relief for a difficult situation when only one family member gains some awareness into the dynamics of the family system. This awareness will, in turn, affect the larger family system.

Each family evolves a social order of its own through years of living together. Unspoken rules, subtle nuances of language, interpersonal relationships—all are part of the complex structure. But individuals change. Their bodies change with age. Their minds and attitudes change as they learn and mature. All of life is in flux. Opportunities arise, crises present themselves and must be resolved. Perhaps no time presents so many challenges as middle age in family life. This period is rife with change: challenges to power and authority, as shown by the reach for independence when children leave home (and hardly predate the time when the husband and wife face transitional periods in their own sexuality and careers); facing menopause and retirement; the dependency and death of parents. Decisions middle-aged people make about the dependency needs of aging family members will be particularly difficult if they have lacked a unified policy in terms of their functions, relationships, roles, and responsibilities toward one another. Yet these problems are often predictable and if anticipated, need not cause more anguish and anxiety than necessary.

The "Life Review"

A son's visits to his mother were becoming increasingly difficult for him and for his family after she had been placed in a nursing home. "She keeps telling me the same stories over and over, without any sense of continuity or point to them. I can't count the number of times she's told me about her pregancy and my birth, about her years as a school teacher before she married my father. It's so unlike her to talk so much about nothing and then to become anxious if she thinks that I'm not listening."

Their relationship had always been close. He was the long-awaited child she thought she might never have. She had married late in life and then devoted herself entirely to her husband and son. She doted on the young boy, and he loved her uncompromisingly, but sometimes wished for more freedom of action away from her. Although she seldom reproached him, he felt that when he was away from her, she blamed him for leaving her alone, although she never said this. As soon as he finished college, he married his childhood sweetheart, and they lived near his parents, visiting often. When his father died, his mother moved to a small apartment a short car ride from his home. He and his wife and children saw her often and enjoyed the time they spent together. Since her heart attack she seemed to change totally. Her son asked the nursing home staff if she was becoming senile, and what could be done about it. It was explained to him that often, when people feel death is drawing closer, they experience a process called the "life review." Recapturing memories of people and events helps to make their world keep shape.

Looking Beyond Behavior

In looking for reasons for his mother's new and seemingly disturbed behavior, the son was better able to tolerate her endless reminiscences. He realized that despite feelings of anxiety and resentment, he also had many pleasurable moments when they were together. As he became more aware of his own feelings, his visits passed more quickly and took on more meaning. He noticed that as he was able to accept her need for him, she in turn became calmer. By the simple act of listening, he helped her to reaffirm her existence.

In the final paragraph of an article, "The View From 80," Malcolm Cowley wrote about remembrances, "It is a fascinating pursuit in itself, and our effort will not have been wasted if they help us to possess our own identities as an artist possesses his work. At least we can say to the world of the future, or to ourselves if nobody else will listen 'I really *was*,' or even, with greater confidence, 'I was and I am *this.*' "

The Masks of Aging:
Equating Old Age with Illness

Many of the assumed masks of aging appear as physical symptoms. Depression, for example, is often masked by a multitude of physical complaints. The older person rarely admits to the doctor, "I am depressed" and then lists various emotional or psychological complaints. Instead she may say, "I feel tired and hopeless because I awake with dizziness and nausea." The doctor in turn does not usually ask about mood or circumstances. Presenting physical complaints further validates what society says to the aging: "You are old, therefore you are sick." Thus, fear and worries that could be allayed become physical symptoms.

Hypochondria is a morbid condition characterized by depression and fancies of ill health concerning the physical functioning of the body or of one of its parts. As with all conditions, it is a matter of extremes. These days many people are very much aware of the functioning of their bodies, and have an almost religious fervor about regular exercise and proper diet. This is now considered normal. However, to the hypochondriac, the relentless pursuit of medical treatment is a basic way of relating to the world. In this way they not only get attention and care from the family, but also from others, such as nurses and doctors.

In women, the onset of hypochondriasis can often occur at a time of change in family role:

- When children leave home and the housewife/mother is no longer needed as before.
- When the husband retires and the spouse relationship is in a new phase.
- After a divorce or widowhood.
- Perhaps during a sudden reemergence of thwarted ambitions from earlier years, and not knowing how to fulfill these ambitions.

For both men and women, the hypochondriacal reaction may also represent unfulfilled sexuality. Since the sick role is more acceptable than the sexual role for older people in our society, hypochondriasis may be a displaced way of focusing on the body, playing out society's expectation of equating old with sick.

Hypochondriasis can be very disruptive of family life, as the following example will illustrate.

The Chronic Complainer

"I get terribly depressed when I'm with my mother, and I stay depressed long after each visit. She talks of nothing but her aches and pains, about what she said to her doctor and what he said to her. Each time I'm at her house she pulls out all her medications and tells me which one is for what and she always says the same thing. I begin to feel sick listening to her. Who wants to hear this? After all, everyone has aches and pains, especially at our ages." He's sixty-two and his mother is eight-one years old. "I've always been close to my parents, and before my father died, I told him I'd take care of Mama. He knew I would. I didn't even have to say it. And now look at me," said Alfred Cantori in distress. "My wife goes to see her, my sister goes to see her, and I can hardly ever get there, and when I do, I think I upset her. You know, I never thought that being a hypochondriac, which is what I think she is, could be so serious," he added.

Symptoms of Needs

The son was not interested in complex explanations or in probing his psyche or his mother's, but he was willing to listen to sensible suggestions. It was obvious that both he and his mother were very distressed by this change in their relationship; his daughter suggested that he consult a family therapist. He was advised by the therapist to try to pay attention to his mother, to listen, to respond, and to accept her as she was, at least for the moment, and perhaps she would become less anxious when they were together. At first he went to see her with his wife or daughter, and these visits went reasonably well for him, although he was not able to say very much to her. But on his first visit alone, he came away with a "terrible feeling" that he was unable to describe. Helped to do so by the therapist, he said he had felt manipulated by his mother, which made him feel angry. His feelings accepted, it was explained to him in broad terms that his mother probably had many unhappy feelings that she could not express, feelings of fear and of inadequacy because she was no longer able to be independent and useful. She is old and without a husband. No one needs her anymore, and she is in pain. This may be why she continually tests her son: "Is he listening to my complaints? Is he aware of my suffering? Will he take care of me?" However, she does not ask him these questions directly. Instead, she says, "This is my liver pill and this is what I take for my heart spasms. The doctor said that if I don't improve I may need an operation." Her behavior is adaptational, which means that it is an appropriate adjustment to a condition. Therefore, confrontation would be harmful and, if anything, would reinforce her feelings that "nobody cares about me." But if her family can make her feel less isolated and more loved and worth loving, they may be able to reawaken her ties to her former life and rekindle old interests that may replace her unhealthy preoccupation with body processes.

All too often in clinical practice, one sees that a problem has existed for a long time and receives attention only when it becomes almost beyond endurance. Sometimes months or even years of suffering could have been spared if attention had been paid sooner. Yet there is a tendency not only among families, but among professionals as well, to ascribe problematic behavior to the normal vicissitudes of aging. "What do you expect of Helen? She's past seventy-seven." Obviously it is better for the older person and for those who care for her to try to find solutions rather than to write her off as hopeless or to ignore her deficits and potentials. Many conditions can be ameliorated, if not cured. Even patients suffering from the progressive, chronic form of dementia can be helped if we reduce the excess disability. The belief that nothing can be done only hastens the progression of the disease.

Similarly, tension and stress increase when the family focuses on a problem behavior, such as hypochondria, which is merely a symptom of the real disturbance. Expecting change to take place in the behavior of a disturbed person at any age, without attempting to understand the relationship between behaviors and symptoms, leads to further feelings of hopelessness. Change should be within the family system, which means that all or at least most members will adapt, not just the "sick" one.

Age Is Not a Deterrent to Treatment

While age is no deterrent to treatment and relief, age is sometimes used as an excuse. To some, the fact that Dad is *old* may to some degree dignify his new and difficult behavior, but this does not make their day-to-day living any easier. Many professionals believe that psychotherapy is not appropriate for the elderly for a variety of reasons: They are too set in their ways; they are too confused or resistant; they do not live long enough to gain the benefits of long-term treatment. Thus, older people do not usually receive individual psychotherapy, but professional literature as well as the author's (MBW) own clinical experience provide many positive accounts. Often, success is achieved with the older person when the traditional focus shifts from placing emphasis upon exploring experiences and feelings to placing more effort into understanding present feelings, circumstances, and relationships. In trying to improve these, limited goals are set; and when they are reached, the next step is planned.

Chapter Eight

Retirement

A person is always startled when he hears himself seriously called an old man for the first time.

Oliver Wendell Holmes, Sr.

The transition from work to retirement is one of the major changes in the later years; frequently, it is a critical period for the individual and the family. To the government of an industrialized society, retirement poses economic problems. To the individual it may pose serious personal problems, for retirement can affect a person's self-image as well as income.

Retirement as a New Phenomenon

Retirement is relatively new to our way of life. Until 1935, when the U. S. Congress passed the Social Security Act, which institutionalized retirement by establishing the minimum age for retirement benefits at sixty-five, only the rich could afford to retire. Other people had to work until ill health or the inability to find employment forced them out of the work place. In the early part of this century there were more small family businesses; more people were self-employed. Therefore, if they could afford *not* to work, they could decide on their own age of retirement, and many switched to part-time work or less demanding work. As a result of present retirement policies, fewer men over the age of sixty-five are now in the work force, whether or not they want to be. In 1900, 68 percent of men over sixty-five were working; by 1960, only 32 percent were employed; by the end of the 1970s, the proportion decreased to 23 percent. In contrast to this, a higher percentage of married women and widows are now in the work force.

Expectations about retirement and its realities often turn out to be quite different.

In his book *The Sociology of Retirement*, R. C. Atchley identified quite separate phases in post-retirement. The first phase is thought to be the honeymoon phase, a euphoric period in which the individual thoroughly enjoys his newly acquired freedoms. The honeymoon phase is followed by a disenchantment phase, a period of dissatisfaction and adjustment problems, perhaps caused by inadequate finances, loss of friends, and loss of occupation. These two phases, it has been suggested, are likely to occur within the first five years after retirement (Hinds, 1963). Of course, this does not apply to everyone.

Health and Well-Being

Recent studies have not found any support for the widespread belief that the stress of retirement results in feelings of rejection and physical or mental ill health. On the contrary, for many working men, the release from the exacting physical labor over long hours *in unsatisfactory conditions* is followed not by frustration and disengagement, but by more enjoyable leisure-time activities, closer family ties, and better physical health. Working men over sixty-five years seem to be generally healthier and better adjusted than retired men, but this is not necessarily because they are working; it is because they are healthy enough to be working. Although it has not been substantiated that retirement causes ill health, there is more evidence to indicate that poor health may be a major cause *for* retirement, particularly before the conventional age of sixty-five.

In a pioneering study of occupational retirement, researchers at Cornell University observed improvement in health after retirement, especially among unskilled workers (Streib and Schneider, 1971). In searching for explanations for this phenomenon, the investigators conjectured that the about-to-retire worker, pushed to his limit to meet the demands of a workday, finds that by contrast, the physical demands of a day's activities *after* retirement are well within his capacity. Consequently, respondents to this study assessed their health more favorably after retirement than before.

Retirement is a complex issue. On the one hand, it has become a normal and expected phase of the life cycle, to be looked forward to, prepared for, and enjoyed. But it is also the retired person's responsibility to find satisfactory ways of ending paid employment, one of the most significant roles in life, without suffering economic hardships or emotional deprivations such as loss of self-esteem, loneliness, and boredom. Preparation for retirement is now a widely recognized need; it is catered to by many voluntary organizations, do-it-yourself books, centers for adult education, and the media. Nevertheless, many people do not face the problem soon enough and enter retirement inadequately prepared.

Self-Esteen: Losses and Gains

For many older men today, work and the work place are the center of their activities and the major source of friendship and identity. They were the breadwinners in the family; they worried about money, decided how it was to be spent, and doled it out to their wives and children without any discussion. Often they are working men one day, and when they wake up the next morning, they are retirees.

"Since he retired, Dad's been driving us all crazy, telling us what to do, then checking up to make sure we've done it. Sometimes I think he completely forgets that I have grown up and am the father of a family of my own," a son said about his sixty-three-year-old father.

This successful energetic man was forced to retire prematurely when the company he worked for was taken over by a conglomerate, and an executive position at his level of experience was not available. Although he had enough money to live comfortably, he was not prepared for the abrupt end to his work life, and felt desperate when faced with the change in the structure in his everyday life. In an effort to remain in a position of control, he began to make demands of his family. When they resisted, he wondered why the world around him had suddenly changed when he had not, and he became depressed.

All his life, he had been rewarded by a society that admires the person who is forceful and dynamic. His reinforcements of money, position, and power in this world have been plentiful. As his rewards for self-assertion and control increased, so too did an underlying anxiety about ambivalent feelings of omnipotence and vulnerability. If he could become aware of these contradictions and allow himself to feel some need for dependency, then it would be easier for him to maintain his balance during this transitional period. But his way of crying out for help made it difficult for his family to be sympathetic. Nevertheless, if the family is to help him overcome his depression and find new involvement in work and leisure, they must respond with patience, concern, and understanding. Being critical and pointing out all the mistakes he is making is obviously counterproductive.

Many large companies provide counseling for prospective retirees, but usually their focus is on practical issues: financial planning, medical care, housing, and the like. However, there are an increasing number of preretirement programs given in adult education centers and university-based gerontology centers where the emotional and social concerns are considered. Because many individuals are pursuing an active life after retirement, this period should be approached as another career at which they have to work.

As previously mentioned, there are people who want to continue working as long as possible, and at the same time there are those who want to leave their jobs as soon as they reach retirement age, or before. There are forces that encourage early retirement and those that argue for extending work life. Numerous studies have been attempted to understand the dual nature of the phenomenon of retirement and its emerging patterns, examining how the characteristics of various retirees and the situations in which they find themselves interact with one another, and how in the long term they may affect the economic and psychosocial life in our society.

Research Findings on Retirement

Beginning in 1969, the Office of Research and Statistics of the Social Security Administration (Department of Health, Education and Welfare [HEW], 1976) selected 11,153 people between the ages of fifty-eight and sixty-three to participate in a ten-year study of the retirement process. Information was collected on their work lives, health, living arrangements, financial resources and assets, expenditures, and retirement plans.

Health status, quite obviously, is of prime importance from the point of view of happiness and satisfaction in retirement. The DHEW study found that most of the preretirement group were in good health, although 13 percent were severely enough impaired to be unable to work; another 10 percent had limiting disabilities which caused them to change jobs. Among the men who did retire early, the most prevalent (65 percent) reason for leaving was poor health. Only 12 percent of those men still working viewed their health as worse than that of others their age, as contrasted with 60 percent of those out of the labor force. It is significant to note that more of the early retirees had held manual jobs as opposed to professional, sales, or managerial positions, a type of job that may have been associated with more potentially hazardous situations, resulting in health limitations.

A related area of concern in retirement is health insurance. Most of the group (78 percent) had some insurance; however, among the uninsured, almost one fifth paid 10 percent or more of their income for health care. This is of some concern, considering that a substantial proportion of this preretirement group has low income. For example, the net worth (defined as worth of remaining assets after subtracting debits) of 10 percent of the group was negative, indicating a risk of poverty in retirement. Moreover, the net worth of those who were unmarried was much lower than that of married individuals.

A self-rating of morale was also obtained: Respondents were asked, "Taking things all together, would you say you're very happy, pretty happy, or not too happy these days?" About half the respondents placed themselves in the "pretty happy" category. This proportion did not differ for the married, the nonmarried men, and the nonmarried women. The proportions indicating that they were "very happy" or "not too happy" did differ substantially, however. One third of the married men, but only about one-fifth of the nonmarried men and women reported that they were "very happy."

Research data as well as common sense tell us that at every stage of life, but more so in retirement, three factors are essential: good health, adequate income, and close interpersonal relationships. But for many people, work also contributes much to basic psychological needs. To men for whom work and the work place have been the primary focus of activity and socialization, retirement is a serious threat to morale and self-concept. Even when they do not like their jobs, a worker's day is structured by routine. Work often provides major social relationships for individuals. Retirement may necessitate devising some other means of finding satisfaction and structure.

In-depth studies of married women in retirement are very few, but it has been suggested that they may be better equipped than nonmarried women or men to cope with the emotional upheaval at the end of their work life because they have had more than one major role to perform. Whether she is a dressmaker or a corporate vice-president, a married woman still has to function in other roles as wife and mother; traditonally, women have anticipated becoming care-giver to aged parents and then to their aging spouse. As more women enter the job market, and there is real crossover in roles, and responsibilities with more equal sharing of child rearing and breadwinning in families, retirement may be easier for both partners. However, retirement poses problems for some women. Single women obviously face similar problems as men, but married women who are working may welcome retirement if they have been doing two jobs, housework and paid employment, for a long time. A woman who has not gone out to work may find her husband's retirement a difficult adjustment to make.

Mental Adjustment: A Case Study

Frank and Anne Harding were married for over thirty-two years when Frank considered retirement. He had always worked hard, and together they had managed their money well so they could save and still give themselves and their sons many of the things they all valued. He and Anne were in their early sixties and in good health when he began to anticipate a more leisurely life. Frank had for some time felt that his middle management job was boring and routine, and he was ready for what he called an extended vacation.

Anne fully understood her husband's yearning for freedom, and felt he had earned it after all his years of hard work. She herself had a great need for autonomy, but had been totally responsible to her family. She was always there when the boys came home from school, and she planned family outings on weekends. As soon as the boys started school, she began to develop a life of her own, first becoming active in the parent-teacher association and then in other community activities, taking courses, and making friends with women who had similar interests. When their sons were in college, she went out to work to help pay the tuition. Her daily routine was tightly organized and very enjoyable. "The days are mine, and nights and weekends I share with my husband. I feel free during the day, coming and going where I want, when I want. The truth is that the thought of Frank being underfoot all day, every day, wanting me to prepare lunch for him and to go out with him, fills me with apprehension."

Frank was looking forward to his days of ease, of breaking old routines. He made long lists of things he wanted to do and places he wanted to see, and expected that Anne also eagerly anticipated his new fredom. Then he sensed her apprehension. Being aware of one another's feelings, and realizing that this decisive change in their lives could easily lead to conflict, they sought counseling. Being a caring and communicating couple, they rather quickly found a middle ground in which to respond to one another's needs while still fulfilling themselves as separate people.

Retirement gives men their first chance to experience, to some degree, the traditional role that many housewives have had, with its autonomy and the inherent responsibility for self-motivation

The Right to Work

In his landmark book, *Why Survive? Being Old in America*, Dr. Robert Butler noted that the right to work is basic to the right to survive, and that, ideally, retirement should be an option based upon the individual's needs and wishes and upon an evaluation of his or her physical and emotional capabilities to function.

As life expectancy increases, and with it the proportion of the elderly, there will have to be more flexibility about age entry into school and into the work force, and less emphasis on role-appropriate behaviors as they relate to chronological age. This flexibility can already be seen among the young, many of whom work for some years between high school and college and then return to complete their education in their late twenties and thirties. Many people in their middle years start second careers. The sharp break between work and leisure can be cushioned with more flexible work hours, part-time work, and second careers, allowing for gradual easing into retirement. Individual needs and past life-styles must be considered so that those in post-retirement remain a productive and integral part of society, sharing a variety of roles, both voluntary and fee-paying. This will have far-reaching implications in terms of de-emphasis on the work ethic and a realization of social values other than those anchored in technology, and it will provide an opportunity for self-actualization (Tibbitts, 1979). As people grow older, these new roles may be less contingent upon actual performance of functions and more related to emotional factors, such as sharing, advice giving, encouraging, and loving.

Chapter Nine

Mourning and Afterward

It is perfectly true, as philosophers say, that life must be understood backwards. But they forget the other proportion, that it must be lived forwards.

Søren Kierkegaard

Families are the result of biological and emotional connections producing a multitude of characteristics that make each family, as each individual, unique. The way in which a family meets the responsibilities and challenges at each stage of life, but particularly at critical periods, is influenced by the tradition, values, and emotional ties that have developed over many years.

Family Stages

Certain basic patterns begin with the birth of a child. Some couples find the day-to-day care of their infant more demanding than they anticipated and seek ways to overcome the constraints that parenthood places on their life-style. The mother returns to work as soon as alternate arrangements can be made for child care. The child goes to a play group as soon as it is ready, spends weekends with friends or grandparents, goes to summer camp. Life is organized and goal-oriented, and both parents so eagerly await each step toward independence that they never fully allow themselves to enjoy the physical contact, dependency, and affection of their child. Results, accomplishment, and self-sufficiency are their goals, and they function best when everything fits into a pattern to allow them to achieve these goals.

To another couple, their child's reach toward independence is seen as threatening. Separation from them is not easily tolerated because they perceive the outside world as potentially dangerous. Sending their child to school creates anxiety for them, as they are in constant fear of desertion and loss of affection through separation. They project these fears to the child, who is often absent from school because of "illness." The parents construct logical excuses to cover the intensity of their need to carry out the family message: "Stay close to me, for I will not be able to tolerate the loss."

Yet despite the restraints, the family system must adapt to the growth of the child, who, nearing adolescence, naturally reaches toward the outside world. New interests, new experiences, new friends must be explored. An integrated family functions rather like an accordian, expanding and contracting with changing needs and external conditions, whereas the members of a tightly defensive family do not allow expression of the full range of their emotions; they seem to continually contract, despite circumstances.

The Fear of Separation

In such a family, the fear of separation may set up limitations that restrict free choice. A son, for instance, is expected to go into his father's business or follow the same profession; a daughter is expected to live close by, even after she marries. "Why don't we buy a house together?" the parents ask, and give many sound reasons for the practicality of their suggestion.

The children of such parents often find themselves in a double-bind situation. If they allow themselves to remain dependent, to let their parents determine their lives in important ways, they can expect to feel angry, bitter, and disappointed. But if they become independent, assertive, and live their own lives, they may feel guilty because they are "deserting" their parents. With the birth of a third generation, some of these patterns of control and behavior will be repeated.

Predictable Patterns

The complex and subtle patterns to which families adhere are frequently indications of how they will function in times of stress, change, and old age. Are they supportive or do they seem to work against the best interests of one another? Are they candid or do they resort to hidden messages? Are they aware of their collective strengths and weaknesses? Can they look realistically at their parents or themselves and anticipate that it will be very difficult for them to adjust to the normal bodily losses of age, such as decreased vision, hearing, and energy; and will they have the resilience to find ways to compensate for these deficits?

Surviving a Death in the Family

Some people, bred in an environment of tight restraints and unrealistic expectations, may react quite differently to the physical deficits of aging, with an attitude that states, "I am old, therefore I cannot take care of myself." They may give in at the first sign of aging, thus capitulating without a struggle. Is it easier for them or for those who struggle against the deficits of old age and death? Of course no one knows, but what we need to learn is how to relate to the dying person, who feels alone mentally, if not physically, and how to allay the suffering of close family members who cannot bear to witness the pain and anguish of terminal illness.

    The children of a dynamic and independent eighty-five-year-old woman admitted that they did not know how to relate to their mother or comfort her during the last months of her life when she was helpless and in severe pain. After she died, they realized that they had spent more time consulting with hospital staff and talking to one another in the hospital corridor outside her room about what medical procedures should be taken than they had spent at her bedside. Her son recalled, "She kept calling to the dead, her parents and my father, begging them to come for her and put an end to her agony. I didn't know whether to tell her that they would come soon, so I just said 'The doctor will give you something to help.' I wish now that I had been more honest. I think she wanted that."

A family's well-being is based upon a sense of interdependence, intimacy, commitment, and its ability to be honest with one another. Adapting to the death of one of its members is its most severe challenge. Watching someone we love dying makes us feel that we too are being drawn into an abyss; when the person is gone, we are still here, to face the powerful emotions within us of grief, anger, guilt, and fear: Will it really happen to me—and when?

Helping the Widowed

While anticipation and preparation help to pave the way for most events in life, and death comes to all, there is no adequate preparation for the losss of a loved one and for widowhood. In comforting the mourner, we need to recognize that we are, in a sense, also comforting ourselves and softening the feelings of interminable loss. Although people express grief in many different ways, it is generally accepted that the period of seemingly inconsolable mourning lasts between three months and one year, although some people may mourn much longer. Part of dealing with this loss may be the attempt to sift out the apparent meaninglessness of the act—"Why did it happen to me? What was it all about? She was so young/good/bright/able." Ultimately, the mourner needs to find a new equilibrium, a way of coping with the sudden empty space death leaves. Regardless of age and how well-seasoned a person is, widowhood is a new experience. After a lifetime shared with a partner, the survivor is suddenly alone. Shared secrets, experiences, conversations are now turned into memories only.

Respect for personal expressions of grief will make this period somewhat easier. For some, solitude is preferred, as they sift through life's experiences and deal with the strangeness now inside them. For others, plunging into activity appears to soothe the pain and hasten the healing. Time is the best thing we can give mourners: time to be by themselves, and time that we will spend with them when they need companionship. In comforting mourners, it is important to recognize the normality of the feelings of loss. This is one way the widowed have of healing themselves.

Loss of a Parent

We are all the children of children; we pass on the values, rituals, flexibilities, and rigidities of generations. "After a certain age, the more one becomes onself, the more obvious one's family traits become," Marcel Proust observed.

As mature adults, we do not have the same relationship with our parents as we did when we were children. However, our desire for the nurturing parent never ceases. When a parent dies, we are suddenly reduced to feeling like a child, abandoned and alone. For no matter at what age it happens, when our parents die, we are no longer somebody's child, however independent or secure we may be.

Adaptation to Living Alone

In our society it is more often the woman who faces the last years of life alone.* Yet often, she is not adequately prepared to cope alone, particularly when her husband's death is sudden

---

*Almost 75 percent of women over the age of 75 are widowed, and 6 out of 10 older widows live alone. The 1980 census shows that among the "young/old," or 65 to 74 age group, there were about 77 men per

and plans have not been made for her future. Among many older couples, the husband is dominant, and even if the wife works outside the home, she relies on him for all major financial decisions. She may have no idea of how to manage money, balance a checkbook, or pay bills. Married women in their seventies and eighties did not usually go out to work. More likely, they were conditioned to accept a certain amount of money to run the house and took no part in financial decision making. While the older male may be deficient in ways of the kitchen, the older woman may be lacking in ways of the checkbook and finances.

With more women in the work force today, open communication about finances represents an important change from the way many women were taught. A seventy-two-year-old widow said that her parents must have discussed money matters, but she certainly did not know when. "And when I married, I didn't even know what a mortgage was. But when I went out to work after the children were grown, my husband was nearing retirement and money management became a serious, if new, discussion between us. Periodically, we updated the discussion about what steps to take if either of us should die in the near future: how much the survivor would have to live on, what changes in life-style would be necessary, and how to change a will. We made the necessary contingencies and felt secure about this, but some people with whom we discussed the idea found it shocking."

Resourceful Living

When there are strict divisions in responsibilities, the death of a spouse represents serious losses in practical terms. When the

---

100 women; for the 75 to 84 age group there were 50 men per 100 women; and for the "old/old," 85 and over, only 44 men per 100 women. Demographic projections for the over-65 population in 1990 state there will be 76.5 men to every 100 women; at age 75 the ratio will be 57.8 men to every 100 women (U.S. Senate Special Committee on Aging Report, 1982; Department of Health and Human Services, Administration on Aging, 1979; National Council on Aging, 1978).

wife dies, the husband loses his cook, housekeeper, and laundress. When the husband dies, the wife loses her business manager, chauffeur, and handyman.

If plans have not been made, children may make hasty decisions for their parent during the initial period of intense grief and bewilderment. One of these decisions may involve living arrangments. Should the new widow stay in the family home or should she move in with a child or go to an adult residence? If she leaves her home, should she stay in the same neighborhood or go elsewhere? A woman who was a widow of a few months told a counselor: "I miss my husband a great deal. I know I'm depressed and that's why I came to see you, but I'm embarrassed to admit another loss I feel. I miss the little front porch in my old apartment. Funny, but it really was my 'window to the world.' All the time Jim was sick, I would sit out on the porch and feel comforted just looking out at the world and the people. Then when I finally came inside, back into the apartment, I could face everything and felt so much calmer. When he died, my daughters and I felt it would be best for me to give up this apartment. It seemed reasonable. I didn't need four rooms anymore. A studio seemed right and was certainly less expensive. But now I don't have my 'window,' and all day I sit alone and feel locked in."

The period of mourning may seem endless to the entire family if the widowed parent is not encouraged to adapt to new, albeit enforced circumstances. Assuming a widower decides to live on his own, he may have to learn housekeeping, shopping, and everyday living skills, while a widow may have to learn to organize her own finances and deal with other tasks often assigned to the male, such as house and car repairs. While the learning of these tasks could seem overwhelming at first, the handling of routine affairs and the development of new skills lead to a sense of achievement. Good feelings from new accomplishments carry over, sometimes even through grief, and help the person by reinforcing feelings of self-esteem and independence. As Dr. Robert N. Butler has stated: "One of the greatest dangers in life is being frozen into rigid roles that limit one's self-development and self-expression. We need to enhance their reality and the sense of personal growth throughout the course of life until its very end." (Butler, 1970, p. 23).

Children think they know their parents, and are sometimes surprised when their seemingly docile, dependent mother displays spirit and determination to lead her own life and have her own way after the death of their father. Conversely, a dominating father who ran everyone's life becomes shattered and almost immobilized in widowhood, unable to cope with the loss of his wife and the new role of providing totally for himself. Sometimes when a woman has spent years taking care of a sick husband, her children may be shocked at what to them seems to be an inappropriately short period of grief for their father, and the widow herself may be surprised at her unexpected sense of relief and freedom. Many widows who provide constant care for a sick husband understandably state that they are apprehensive about remarriage, lest they have to become nurse to a sick older man once again. However, not just loneliness, but feelings of extreme emptiness and isolation may overwhelm the individual living alone after years of shared experiences and activities. The obvious way to avoid loneliness is to seek the company of others, but the death of a spouse changes one's social status, and this can affect relationships. In our society, the widower's social position remains more secure than the widow's. An extra man is made to feel welcome and prospective partners are quickly found for him, as there are so many more older women than men. But a woman alone is not always welcomed. Even close friends may feel that widows bear a special burden of self-pity and tend to avoid her. Her close friends may consider her a threat to their marriages, and their husbands may not want to see her because her presence reminds them of their own vulnerability to death. Superficial factors can become handy excuses for everyone. The widow feels a certain awkwardness about social amenities which were once taken for granted: Should she call the couple (and which of the two?), or should she wait for them to invite her out to dinner or to a movie? And friends wonder if they should let her pay when they go out together, and if they should pick her up and take her home after they have taken her out. These details can of course be easily resolved by frank discussion, but often none of these considerations are even mentioned, and contact becomes less frequent. The breakup of old friendships can be another of the losses in widowhood.

Sexuality in the Later Years

Often women find it more comfortable to seek the company of other women rather than couples where each of the three people are not sure of their roles. However, the companionship of other women may not alleviate lonely feelings. Some feel alone even when surrounded by others because these relationships may lack intimacy. Moreover, while women need other women as confidantes and companions, the majority of women also seek sexual companionship from a male. This is particularly true when the couple enjoyed their sexual lives together and where the woman did not spend a great deal of time caring for an ailing husband. Where there was prolonged caring, many widows have stated that they are apprehensive about a new relationship with a man, fearing that once again they will have to become nurse and care-giver.

When a woman does seek a mate in the later years, it is generally assumed that she is lonely and looking for companionship only. In these permissive, sex-conscious days, sexuality in old age is viewed not only as incongruent, but perverse. However much both older men and women are considered asexual, the sexual interests and appetites of men are tolerated much longer than those of women. Once past menopause—or even sooner, according to media images—a woman's sexual appetite vanishes and she is relegated to a rocking chair, where only passive rocking-chair habits are considered appropriate.

This stereotype has been so pervasive that young and old alike have almost unquestioningly accepted it. One reason suggested by some researchers (Starr and Weiner, 1981) is that a dormant Oedipal situation may be reactivated, and a middle-aged child may deny that his widowed parent "does that." This reaction can be expressed in subtle ways: A daughter tells her counselor "my mother's boyfriend is clearly after her money," or the son states "Mother must be senile or she wouldn't be going out with him . . . and doing all sorts of things." His blush and embarrassment conclude the thought he is unable to express.

Despite stereotypes and assumptions that sexually active older people are the exception, recent data suggests otherwise. For example, a recent questionnaire survey of eight hundred older Americans living in communities throughout the country revealed that a large majority of the participants said they were sexually active, that they enjoyed sex, and that they held more liberal views about sexuality than popular notions suggest (Starr and Weiner, 1981). The authors concede that those with sexual interests were undoubtedly more likely to participate in the survey, but that this limitation (to generalizability) does not detract from the phenomenon of sexuality in the later years. They suggest that this is an extremely hopeful report for people of all ages, especially middle-aged people who think their sex lives will soon be over. The study supports suggestions from previous research that an important predictor of an active sexual life in old age is sexual activity throughout the preceding years (Butler and Lewis, 1977).

Limitations to Sexuality for the Older Woman

The scarcity of older men is another significant factor in the limitation of sexual activity among older women. Some respondents to the Starr-Weiner questionnaire stated that they would seek, or have already sought, other means of sexual satisfaction, including masturbation, sharing of men, and lesbianism. A large proportion said that they sublimate sexual desire by involving themselves in work, hobbies, travel, their families, and in building tender, loving relationships with other older women.

While a man of any age can attract a partner, and usually a younger partner if this is his desire, older women have learned to accept that they have little or no sexual attraction for men, yet age does not protect them from desire or the pangs of unobtainable love.

The reward for a long life is old age, but for many older people—women particularly—the final years can become a time of segregation and isolation. We know how retirement can disrupt living habits when little organized counseling or education is given. Too often, no serious consideration is given to planning a new life after the death of a spouse, when suddenly the survivor has much time free of responsibility, of work, and of structured duties. What should widows do after a lifelong commitment to others? We have not yet discovered the full answer, but one direction lies in helping them to move in the further use of their skills; the possibility of part-time employment and volunteer activities; and, when they have no families of their own, of developing friendships and surrogate roles, if old age is to be more than just a waiting time.

Chapter Ten

The Young/Old

Grow old along with me!
The best is yet to be,
The last of life, for which the first was made.

Robert Browning ("Rabbi Ben Ezra")

The Elderly Are a Diverse Group

Characteristics are as different between twenty-five-year-olds and forty-five-year-olds as they are between people of sixty-five and those of eighty-five. Why then should sixty-five-year-olds and eighty-five-year-olds be classed together? Older people are no longer a small homogenous group. The physical and mental changes that come with age are varied and do not necessarily develop at the same time in each person. One individual may be tired and listless at sixty-five while another is vigorous and active at eighty-five. And this is a key difference. Bernice Neugarten, a noted gerontologist who has specialized in developmental stages and aging, distinguishes between the "young/old," whatever their age, who are well and functioning without help or with only minor assistance, and the "old/old" who are frail and dependent. However, statistically, the majority of young/old are in the age bracket of sixty-five to seventy-five; while more of the old/old, in terms of functioning are over age seventy-five.

It is important to recognize the distinctions between normal aging, when the hair grays, the skin loses its elasticity, and the body gradually begins to wear down, but the individual is still fit and well, and problem aging, which arises out of disease and disability. When we recognize this distinction, we will be able to overcome the erroneous belief that to turn sixty-five puts one on the borderline between health and illness, and causes an inability to relate to others.

To understand aging as a biological process and growing old as a social process leads to many fields of study. Until the late 1950s, however, little methodical research examined the later years of life and this, according to Dr. Robert Butler, was to a great extent based on studies of institutionalized older men in pathological decline. When independent older people living in the community were studied, findings indicated that the subjects were physically well, psychologically satisfied, and well able to adapt to the many and inevitable changes that occurred in their lives.

Research gives us clues to important questions. The aim of gerontological research is to uncover generalizations about the behavior and functioning of older people in order to evaluate their needs and plan knowledgeably for them and for future generations.

There is no denying the realities of aging, but a positive approach recognizes and separates the aging process from diseases and other factors that cause problems. For example, when the National Institute of Health conducted studies of human aging in the 1950s, people thought of arteriosclerosis as a normal part of aging. Today, we know that it is a disease; and we know that what is too commonly called senility is also a disease (see Chapter 3) that afflicts only a small percentage of the older population.

The mere fact that there are about 26 million Americans over the age of sixty-five leads to a vast range of characteristics among them. To look separately at the two groups, at the young/old and at the old/old, not only helps to give a clearer picture of their different potentials and needs, but also helps to prepare for the transition from one stage to the next.

Aging Does Not Mean Disengagement

Throughout our lives we adapt to new situations and roles. Perhaps no time offers as many challenges as older adulthood. A multitude of new and often stressful situations face the older person: retirement and decline in income, physical decrements, loss of family and friends. To cope with these events, an older person must continually adapt, find opportunities to make new friends, develop new interests, strengths, and resiliencies. Contrary to the image of bored and disengaged "senior citizens" sitting in rocking chairs waiting for their children to call, most older people manage their lives quite well in the face of the many major pressures confronting them. Yet, at the same time, they may also be experiencing the good things that can come with growing older, including ego gratification, tranquility, and wisdom. They have learned what they want and what they do not want, and they can be frank about it.

Older adults who are in good mental and physical health are considered exceptions, but they are in fact not so much more unusual than fit younger people. The body does not become sick, frail, and weak simply because it reaches mandatory retirement age. Biological changes associated with adult life occur gradually. One slows down in old age, and certain adjustments have to be made for this and for illness, but activity does not and should not cease. It is difficult to specify precisely what aging is. If any one assessment could be made, it may be the cumulative ill effects of damage and disease that accompany an inevitable wearing-out process. The senses become less acute; there is loss of vigor and of stature; the muscles grow weaker, but regular exercise helps to maintain their elasticity. The enjoyment of sexual activity is certainly possible for older men and women, and ought to be considered natural even if engaged in less frequently than before, and by bodies that to the young may no longer hold erotic appeal. Recent evidence indicates that frequency may be in less decline than was once believed, and that healthy older people do not lose their enjoyment of sexuality, but for those who never enjoyed lovemaking, or for those with low sex drives or who are ill, old age may become a reason to stop altogether (Starr and Weiner, 1981).

What Do You Expect at Your Age?

Many of the normal deficits that occur with aging, especially those that begin to be noticed by people in their sixties, will not seriously affect their functioning or abilities, unless the deficits are allowed to affect their self-image and social relationships. The homely adage, "You are as old as your arteries," seems to be based on scientific evidence and common sense, as mental status often depends on the condition of the arteries, while social status will often depend on mental performance.

Changes within the brain and the motor systems may decrease the speed with which nerve impulses are carried, so reaction time is slower. Thus, older people may not perform well when rapid responses are called for, but when the pace of learning a task is slowed, their performance improves considerably. With maturity and experience comes a greater conceptual grasp, so older people are able to size up a situation and then refer to the relevant items in their memory and relate to them.

When standing still, older people tend to sway back and forth more than younger people, because their balancing mechanisms become less accurate. Nevertheless, there are many older bicycle riders, skaters, and skiers, which suggests that skills learned early and practiced continually become fundamental and are often well preserved.

Older people need more time to switch from one movement to another, such as from forward to backward, because of a slowdown in psychomotor coordination. In tests that distinguish between speed and timing, it has been shown that they will perform efficiently if the tasks are presented at a somewhat slower rate.

When intelligence tests are used for assessment, older people generally perform less well on tasks that are not relevant to their fields of experience. One of the more commonly used tests, the Wechsler Adult Intelligence Test (WAIS), was standardized on young subjects. Older people score lower on such subtests as block design, picture arrangement, and digit symbol than they do on the vocabulary, information, and comprehension subtests, which have more relevancy to them. Comparing the test scores of young and old led to the erroneous belief that there is a decline in intelligence and performance with age, until other factors were considered (Jarvik and Cohen, 1973). People in their sixties and seventies were not as well educated as those in their twenties and thirties, and they lacked the experience and motivation for test taking. Their anxiety and low expectations may also have contributed to their slow responses. Outstanding achievements in mathematics, biology, and physics are more apt to be made by people in their twenties and thirties than by those in their sixties, but in areas where experience and conceptualization are significant, such as politics, administration, and the arts, achievement is not necessarily affected by age.

There are studies to support the belief that intelligence declines with age, and there are studies to disprove this theory. Nevertheless, it is generally agreed that if people are basically intelligent, and if they do not contract certain kinds of disease in later life, their faculties will normally remain intact. Even if their thought processes change somewhat, they learn shortcuts to solve common problems.

History Influences the Way We Are

Whether the young respond differently than older people to events in their lives is a much-explored area of social and psychological gerontology, using such methods as controlled observations, field research, participant-observer research, large-scale surveys, and analysis of census data. As these data get integrated and reinterpreted, much is learned about social change and generational differences by comparing attitudes of people of various ages at various points in time. These studies help to refute the widely held belief that the process of growing up and growing old must inexorably follow a set pattern. We can now see that each new generation is marked by the imprint of its time and, in turn, leaves its own imprint for the future. The lives of people who grow old in future decades will be different from those of people who are old now. Striking differences can already been seen between the young/old who are sixty and seventy years old and their eighty- and ninty-year-old parents.

People over the age of eighty were members of large extended families. Their lives began in an era when things had been done in much the same way for centuries, and continued to the present, when few things are done as they once were. They are survivors. They have lived through two world wars, through periods of depression, recession, unemployment, and inflation. Retirement came to many of them in the 1960s, a dazzling period of economic affluence and technological growth, when the pensions they received were proportionately lower than those of today. Thus, they have a circumscribed view of their rights and hesitate to make demands on society.

Their children, for the most part, had smaller families and greater expectations. Survival was no longer a fundamental issue, as mortality rates are lower and death more frequently comes at the end of a long life. They are among the first generations to have the time and the money and the inclination to learn how to grow old as they learned how to grow up, with hope and anticipation.

As people move through different stages of life, they gain altered perceptions of themselves, depending upon personal experience. A boy of five will respond differently to his parents' divorce than a boy of fifteen or a married man in his twenties. Personal experience is also influenced by history and social change. A young man looking for his first job during the Depression of the 1930s will have different expectations than a young man going out into the world of the affluent 1960s.

Personality and Life Events

Both common sense and survey data suggest that the main sources of well-being are family life, health, friendship, and financial security. However, it is a prevailing view in social gerontology that age identity is closely related to a sense of well-being or life satisfaction, but this does not mean that only those who feel young will also feel good about themselves. Some people enjoy living and get better and better at it, while others, regardless of age, feel isolated and disengaged from the world around them.

In an effort to identify what most threatens security and well-being at various ages, information was collected from young, middle-aged, and elderly individuals about various life situations and about their feelings of uselessness.

For young men (eighteen to thirty-four), unemployment and loneliness were most detrimental in relation to feeling useless.

For both young and middle-aged women, unemployment and loneliness did not have as depressing an effect on their self-esteem as did lack of income. Lack of education and poor health were also ranked high as causes of dissatisfaction among middle-aged women.

Ill health, loneliness, and loss of influence and control, in that order, were greater worries to older survey respondents than were unemployment or lower income. Loneliness was a key factor affecting self-esteem and life satisfaction (Mutran and Burke, 1979).

The New Breed of Older People

In other surveys, healthy older people stated that they would prefer to put up with fewer comforts, less living space, and even with a certain measure of financial insecurity in order to be independent and in control of their own environment. A direct correlation has been noted between independence and high morale among the elderly. Most healthy older people (about 90 percent) do not live with a child. As many as 70 percent of older adults live in their own homes. When divorce or prolonged unemployment create problems for them, children will move back to their parents' home. It is not unusual for young married couples to move near where the wife's mother lives. Among the young/old and their families, there is an exchange of services, of advice giving, housekeeping, child care, help during illness, and money and gift giving. Among the middle classes, more financial aid may be given by the older generation to the younger family. Many women in their fifties and sixties are in the work force. Moreover, they have interests and activities they enjoy, and no longer fear the empty-nest syndrome, but welcome it, and may even resent frequent impositions of the younger generation on their time and energy.

This is the "new breed of old people," according to Maggie Kuhn, the septagenarian founder of the Gray Panthers. "There are more of us alive today than at any time in history. We are better educated, healthier, with more at stake in this society. We are redefining goals, taking stock of our skills and experience, and looking to the future." Maggie Kuhn set to work organizing the Gray Panthers, the activist group for older people, after she was dismissed from her job as a magazine editor on her sixty-fifth birthday in 1970, when that was the mandatory age for retirement.

This new breed of young/old are a diverse group. They may be widowed, or several times divorced, or never married. They may be rich or poor. Perhaps during their lives they were both rich and poor. They may be pursuing second careers, or doing voluntary work, or enjoying leisure activities. Some manage to do all three at the same time, if this had been the pattern of their lives. They may do a great deal to help others, or do nothing at all, not even for a spouse. They are individuals with a full complement of human frailties, strengths, and idiosyncrasies. Among them are people who were active in social and political issues, who had strong feelings of excitement and vision about improving the world and facilitating happy and healthy life-styles for everyone. Now, as mature adults, when they discover ways in which they do not fit into the "brave new world" they helped to create, they continue in their efforts to do something about it. Statistics indicate that older voters consistently turn out at the polls in greater numbers than the young.

Already we can see how this fastest-growing segment of the population is beginning to affect every aspect of business, medicine, education, leisure, and housing. The business world is always sensitive to the changes in habits, attitudes, and demography of our population; it is now looking to middle-aged and older consumers as a viable market, whereas in the recent past the main target had been the young. Business reports note that with fewer children born and more of them with relatively affluent grandparents, more money per child will be available to spend on toys, books, clothing, and other luxuries. Cosmetics companies show strong interest in selling their products to older women by introducing such items as wrinkle creams, sun creams for protection, stockings to hide crepey legs, and hair dyes for a young look. Studying the population in terms of demographic characteristics such as age, income, education, and occupation is still the most widely accepted marketing tool. Thus, there is some danger that the "new image" coming into advertising and marketing may be another set of clichés, just as misleading as the old stereotype, and another denial of the natural course of growing up and growing old.

With a realistic approach to their needs and potentials, the lives of most older people can be improved and expanded in many ways that are more than just cosmetic. Some enlightened companies have already begun to initiate this via policies that cushion the sharp break between work and leisure, with more flexible work hours, part-time work, and second-career training, allowing for gradual easing into retirement. As life expectancy increases, there will have to be less emphasis on chronological age and more flexibility about age entry into school and out of the work force. Throughout their lives, people should be able to weave in and out of various roles as student, volunteer, worker, and care-giver. The advantages of this flexibility are already apparent among the young, who seem to have no constraints about working or idling for a few years before continuing their education.

Housing is a major area where flexibility and planning are urgently needed. The older population represents a valuable market which builders and architects are eager to tap, yet they rarely respond to their particular needs. The main thrust in retirement housing in the past twenty years has focused mainly on one period of retirement, the early years, when the individual is fit and active. The most functional schemes, however, offer a combination of perfectly normal accommodations with an unobtrusive range of medical and other facilities that may be needed later. The design and concept of retirement housing have not expressed enough versatility. Too often, houses are built on too many levels, with too many steps, inadequate storage space, and poorly planned living space for people who may suffer physical disabilities. Independence can be prolonged if certain accommodations are made in advance: bathroom doors that are wide enough for wheelchairs to pass through, bathtubs with grab bars and a twenty-four-hour emergency alarm system; light switches that are easily accessible; compact kitchens with low, open shelves; furniture that enables the individual to remain active by easing movement. Additional accommodations can be discreetly integrated into the design elements so they are not a constant reminder of special needs, but at the same time address the fact that active retired people may one day need these facilities and will be prepared when the time comes.

Chapter Eleven

The Frail Elderly

*If I could cry, I'd cry,
But I am too old to be anybody's child.*

Stanley Kunitz, *The Quarrel*

The longer we live, the longer we risk sickness and accidents. In old age, or senescence, resistance to disease decreases and healing takes longer, illnesses become more acute, and medical expenses escalate. This is the part of life, or the parting with life, that we most fear for ourselves and for those we love. Seeing someone we know and love who is in pain and drawing close to death creates a sense of helplessness, frustration, and anger, and also forces us to confront our own mortality, our own vulnerability to sickness and death.

In this chapter we will look at how families react in this situation. We will consider the changes in the concept of "burden"; we will examine how families cope with the day-to-day care of their frail elderly relatives; and we will also try to understand how the dependent older person feels at this last stage of life and what can be done to make a long and painful exit easier for all to endure.

Becoming Dependent

Not surprisingly, when the balance shifts from independence to dependency in a relationship, unspoken resentments and existing tensions become magnified. Care givers may be unsure of what to do or how their actions will affect the sick person, and they may feel themselves become overwhelmed, frightened, depressed, and angry by the continual demands made on their time and services. It is equally difficult for the sick person to cope with the complicated feelings that arise because of sickness and dependency, and often his or her frustrations are directed at the care-giver.

The late Dr. Alvin Goldfarb, who many in the field call the father of geriatric psychiatry, defined the dynamics of dependency in old age as multiple loss leading to loss of resources; decreased mastery; and feelings of helplessness which in turn lead to fear, anger, and a search for help (Goldfarb, 1965). He maintained that psychological dependency was not suddenly acquired in the later years, but represented a behavior which became more visible in old age when physical needs and loneliness made it more noticeable.

The dependency of adults is not easily tolerated in a society based on rugged individualism and self-sufficiency. We expect a child to be dependent and prepare and plan for the years of care required, but we do not expect this of older people, because it is not totally predictable. We do not know for certain that an older loved one will live long enough to be dependent, and even then, we are not absolutely certain that she will in fact become dependent upon us. Always there is an element of denial.

At eighty years, a woman who all her life had been the proverbial tower of strength was still dynamic and able enough to take care of her bedridden husband and do all the housework this entailed. Her children and grandchildren visited frequently and were prepared to help, but she would not allow them to. She was becoming increasingly irritable and admitted to them that their father was becoming more demanding and difficult, and she seemed to them to be less able to cope than usual, but they attributed much of this to her age. Although they all realized she could not go on indefinitely in this way, no other arrangements were discussed.

She had felt ill for some time but never spoke of it, nor would she see a doctor until the pain she suffered became acute.

By the time she learned that she had cancer, the disease was too advanced for surgery or any other treatment to be effective. Within a short time she became bedfast and incontinent. "Only the pain makes me sometimes forget how unendurable it is to become more dependent than a baby," she cried, and seemed to turn all her energy to dying. Her life ended a few months after the condition was diagnosed. Her husband died a few days later. During those months, their children had to take complete control of their lives and make many hasty decisions that left them uncertain and almost incapable of relating to their parents at their time of greatest need.

Coping with Emergencies

Whether the onset of a crisis is sudden or gradual, families are often unprepared for the emergency and unaware of appropriate agencies, physicians, and other health professionals from whom to seek advice. Plans made during the early stages are usually short-term, involving acute-care hospitals, medical diagnosis, or psychiatric assessment. There may be a decision for the older person to move in with a child or other relative temporarily. There is much to consider, particularly with chronic illnesses, because it is not always possible to determine whether a short stay in a protected environment is all that is necessary. For instance, a seventy-two-year-old woman had severe arthritis but lived alone and managed to take care of herself until one winter, when the condition became so painful that she needed help with the everyday tasks of shopping, cleaning, and cooking. Not wanting to feel dependent on friends and neighbors, she gave up her rent-controlled apartment and went into a nursing home. The following spring she felt better, but had to stay on because it was too difficult and too costly for her to find alternative living arrangements.

In her case, medically oriented housing would have made her daily living more manageable and her life more tolerable. Some older people with functional disabilities can remain in a familiar environment and take care of their basic needs if adequate services for meals and activities, for chiropody and physical therapy are available. Elderly married couples less frequently require admission to long-term residential care because the strengths of one partner often complement the weaknesses of the other. A crippled husband and a partially sighted wife, using their combined skills, can manager their lives in a planned environment.

Alternative Living Arrangements

Between 1968 and 1973, a government-subsidized housing project designed for physically impaired older people was the focus of a study in which 100 residents of this housing project were matched for similarities in terms of age, health status, and functional ability with 100 people living in other types of accommodations (Sherwood et al., 1973). Findings showed that at the end of the five-year period, those living in the Highland Heights project, as it is called, spent significantly less time in long-term-care facilities and were less likely to be institutionalized (thirty-nine compared with fifty-six), and fewer in the housing project group had died (forty-seven to sixty-one).

The Family as Primary Care-Giver

Many chronically ill older people can and do make adjustments to their environment and disabilities. What needs to be learned is what they are able to do in practical terms. Can they sit down and stand unaided? Can they use a knife and fork? Can they get into their clothes without help? Can they get to the toilet alone? Determining what they can do rather than what they cannot do is a more positive and productive approach toward building upon whatever abilities remain and how these can be developed, whether they live with their families or in a nursing home.

Families remain the main provider of help for the frail elderly, and it is often said that if there was a full demand for available social welfare services, probably no government in the world would have sufficient resources to meet the requests. For the most part, other older people and daughters are the caregivers to the chronically ill spouse, parent, or sibling. They try very hard to care for them in their homes far past the point where they are burdensome. This fact is well documented in research literature, and it is also stated that health professionals often do not sufficiently handle the needs of family members during decision-making time, but leave them with the problem of caring for the older person and of finding help while their own health and financial resources decline.

Dealing with Bureaucracy

"You know, it's the damnedest thing—here we are willing to take care of my wife's eighty-three-year-old sister and keep her with us, but they'd rather have her go into a home where she'd get less attention, at three times the cost. All we want is a reimbursement for home help. I've talked to them down at social services many times, but all they say is try to get the law changed."

This man's frustration reflects a problem families often encounter when they try to enlist outside services to keep a sick or disabled person out of an institution. Even when they are able to determine where to go to attempt to get help, they are often met with a bureaucratic system that may seem almost impenetrable. This unnecessary frustration heightens whatever negative feelings already exist regarding the care of elderly dependents.

American families express a willingness to provide support—and they do, in fact, give a great deal of help—but this willingness is not always matched with government assistance. It is here that we can see the effects of the striking differences between the humane attitude of individuals toward their elderly kin and the pervasive societal attitude of prejudice and benign neglect toward the aged in general. Not until we begin to deal with these ambiguous attitudes will we be able to sort out some of the major problems in the regulation of our health-care system.

In Britain and in many European countries, care of the elderly is considered and financed as a *social* service, whereas in the United States this care is approached as a *health* service, a difference that has had striking effects on family care-giving as well as on the length of time that a frail elderly person can remain in the community or must spend in an institution. When there are more community-based supports—such as visiting doctors, nurses, therapists, and social workers—families are less burdened, and some are more willing to keep a sick person at home.

Valuable information on this subject is provided by a landmark study of care-giving conducted by Grad and Sainsbury in England in the 1960s.

A particularly relevant section of the study examined the effects that mentally ill patients have on their families when they are cared for at home. Over a two-year period, more than four hundred families were interviewed in terms of the effects on their work, leisure, income, health, and relations with their neighbors. As in all control studies, basic characteristics were closely matched. The families lived in Chichester and Salisbury, communities chosen for their many similiarities and because the medical and social facilities were comparable, but differed in the way the services were deployed. Chichester had more community-based services, whereas in Salisbury, admission to hospital was more common for similar problems. Throughout the study, it was noted that Chichester families kept their patients at home more often than those in Salisbury. Initially the Chichester families appeared to have more problems to contend with, but over the two-year period it seemed that if success is measured in terms of helping families work out ways of overcoming the day-to-day problems of caring for a patient at home, the Chichester system of regular visits from a social worker who provided practical assistance and supportive psychotherapy had more value in the long run than did the Salisbury system of temporary hospitalization. However, the authors stressed that community care is viable only when combined with extra services and help to the family.

How Long Can Families Continue to Cope?

Many cogent arguments for and against home care for the severely impaired have arisen out of studying the characteristics of institutionalized older patients and their families. For instance, there is evidence that elderly people with family support who enter institutions are in a more deteriorated state than those who go in without kin, indicating that families are caring for their elderly up to the point of very severe impairment (Dunlop, 1980). It is not known, however, whether families may already be providing as much help as they are willing and able, so that perhaps increased allocations for community-based services will not result in more older people being cared for in the home. Research indicates that when the family is temporarily relieved of the burden of care by hospital placement, each time the chronically ill patient returns home, the family is less willing to continue to provide care, particularly with inadequate social supports.

Although American families provide the primary support for the impaired elderly, and they enlist outside services as well, this formal network may not be enough to keep the person out of an institution at the point when that person is too impaired for any care short of that given around the clock. Eugene Litwak, a sociologist who has done extensive work in the area of family networks, suggests that this type of protracted care is provided only at great cost to the family and to formal community supports; so that at this point, a family may be persuaded that a long-term-care facility is the most suitable care giver.

The Institution and the Person

Among nursing home residents, a disproportionate number (71 percent) are women. (Of the entire over-sixty-five population, 59 percent are women; 50 percent are widows.) The typical woman referred for nursing home placement is white, widowed or never married, living alone, and lacking family supports. The plight of the typical older woman confined to a nursing home is vividly described in a letter sent anonymously to a newspaper (*International Herald-Tribune*, October 4, 1979). The letter was written by an eighty-four-year-old woman and signed, "A Prisoner of Neglect." In it she stated that her only crime was having a chronic illness. She had severe arthritis and had broken her hip. While recuperating in the hospital, she realized that she would need special home care, but there was no one she could ask for help. Her husband and only child had died years before. Her nieces and nephews visited her occasionally but she couldn't ask them to take her in, and the few friends she still had were struggling to get by themselves. So she went to a nursing home.

Her description of this home is Dickensian. Due to understaffing, little attention was paid to the comfort of the patients. They had no choices of what to eat or when to eat or when to be bathed. At eight o'clock every evening they were put to bed. A doctor saw them once a month for a few minutes. The physicians who went there didn't notice whether their patients' bodies were foul-smelling or whether their fingernails were trimmed. She had been there five years when she wrote the letter, saying that she felt as if she had been confined to prison and the only way she lived through each long day was with memories of her childhood. She recalled how she used to bake cakes and pies and cook for her family and friends, and she ended the letter by stating, "I pray every night that I may die in my sleep and get this nightmare of what someone has called life over with."

This is an image that may come to the minds of many people when they think about nursing homes. Of course, not all nursing homes are like this, but even if it were the only one, it is still too many. The range of care in nursing homes varies greatly. One factor often associated with high-quality care in a warm and friendly atmosphere seems to be the personality of the administrator in charge. (See Chapter 6 on Nursing Home Placement.)

As many as half of nursing home patients never have a visitor, friend, or relative who might complain on their behalf. People typically enter nursing homes as private patients and then go on to Medicaid when their savings run out. After that transition, they may be unable to change nursing homes, since many homes will not take in anyone who does not enter as a private patient. Generally, there is a waiting list for beds, particularly in homes known for good care. The need is so great that this is not an industry where competition for the consumer's dollar can be counted on to insure good service. Also, conditions in a nursing home can go very bad, very rapidly, making it essential that visitors be vigilant and that there be strict government regulations on inspection.

Running a nursing home is a very difficult business. Recruiting and managing a staff who will efficiently and humanely perform tasks that most of us would not be willing to do is one of the most pressing problems. Yet there are many in which patients are professionally supervised and kept alert and socially involved.

A man, paralyzed from the waist down, incontinent, barely able to feed himself, is president of the residents' council in his nursing home. He chairs the monthly meetings and is the person to whom many go when they have worries or complaints. "In earlier life, I was involved in trade union activity and was chairman of the grievance committee," he said.

What was meaningful to him then is meaningful to him still. His sense of mastery and ability to exercise control over his environment is evident in his restricted but significant activities in the nursing home. Age and the limits imposed by conditions beyond one's control need not put an end to growth and personal achievement.

In facing the problems of, say, a stroke victim, which are not only physical but psychological, attention should be given to rehabilitation as well as merely to custodial care, in order to encourage some independence for as long as possible. Telling the family what needs to be done and directly involving them in the procedures of speech and physical therapy with the patient not only helps the patient and allows staff to get on with other tasks, but can ease the tedium that many visitors to nursing homes feel, and can make them feel that their time there is well spent.

Programmed activities for the elderly in an institutional setting have sometimes been criticized for their seeming lack of purpose or benefit, but these activities are designed to improve physical and mental skills, to provide motivation, to keep patients physically active, and to prevent boredom and isolation by bringing them together as a group. Bingo, for example, may help improve memory while integrating sight, sound, and thinking skills. Singing not only provides enjoyment, but strengthens the lungs, eyes, and ears. Arts and crafts not only have therapeutic value for visually impaired people, but there is a sense of accomplishment and improved self-esteem in working with the hands and making small objects which they can give to their visitors, when they may have so few tangible things to give any more.

What Ever Happened to the Concept of Wisdom in Old Age?

A ninety-year-old woman, who had outlived her husband and only son, decided when she was in the hospital for short-term treatment that she would go to a nursing home instead of trying to live on her own any longer. With the help of her two granddaughters, she found a good facility in her neighborhood. Among her physical problems are arthritis and pernicious anemia. She is also legally blind and hard of hearing. People have often asked her which is worse, not to be able to see or not to be able to hear, and she replies, "They are always surprised when I say not to be able to hear, unless one is born blind. But I lived to nearly eighty-five before I lost my sight, and I have all the memories of beautiful things I've seen, the colors and people's faces, and I have a very vivid recall of all of that. But when one is constantly with other people, it is important to relate to them—and in order to relate to them, you must hear what they are saying. It is a very serious problem. You can't hear, and it's a nuisance to say I don't hear. If I didn't have this tremendous will to live and to know what's going on and to be a part of life, I would withdraw too, and become 'senile' as many around me do."

Hearing aids are difficult to adjust and they amplify all noises. They work best in a one-to-one conversation, when the amplifier is turned up, but in a roomful of people it is difficult to hear at all, and many people turn the hearing aid off—and stop communicating.

Many older people can and do make adjustments to their environment and disabilities. This remarkably vital woman said that instead of insisting that people speak louder, she gets very close to them, and when she gets very close to many of her co-residents, they kiss her, thinking that is why she has done it.

Medical Attitudes Toward the Elderly

Individual personalities and life-styles should be considered in understanding the older person and the family. This is particularly true of reactions to illness. Generally, when an older person faces a serious medical problem, the family doctor is consulted, and that quickly leads to a series of visits to four or five doctors, one for each ailment. There is a heart and a foot and an eye doctor, as well as a surgeon or an internist. It is rare for any of these doctors to consider the overall health problems of the older person or to coordinate their drug regimens. To make matters worse, many of these physicians have a negative attitude toward dealing with older patients.

Dr. Robert Butler has pointed out that even though the elderly make up 40 percent of physicians' office patients, most doctors know little about the specific problems of treating geriatric patients. The study of geriatrics is still among the least popular courses in medical schools. This attitude may relate to the medical emphasis on curing rather than rehabilitation or treatment of chronic diseases. In teaching hospitals particularly, the rarer the disease, the higher the priority and the more attention an "interesting" patient is given.

Older patients are not particuarly interesting or popular. Their complaints often go unheard, even by their doctors. They are given drugs which may, in combination, produce diminished effects or compounding effects, since they often have different doctors treating them for different conditions, and it is not unusual for them to be taking several potent prescription drugs on a regular basis. Dosages and purposes for drugs are not always explained to them, and it is not uncommon to be told, when asking an older person about the drugs she takes, "I don't know what the names are . . . but here, I'll get the bottles. Why do I take them? Well, one is for my heart, I think, and I have to take water pills."

The average person over sixty-five takes thirteen prescription drugs a year. One study showed that seventy- and eighty-year-olds experienced twice as many adverse drug reactions as forty- to fifty-year olds. The side effects are sometimes mistaken for symptoms of a new disorder, prompting the writing of yet another prescription; in other cases, drug-induced effects mimic the symptoms of senility.

An active, self-sufficient woman of seventy was admitted to a nursing home when she broke her hip. She was placed on a daily dosage of medication that included tranquilizers, an antidepressant, and a sleeping pill. Within a few weeks, she became "confused," "paranoid," and, according to a staff report, "in no condition to be left alone."

Her daughter decided to take her out of the nursing home and away from the medication. Within a relatively short time she became mentally alert again.

Drugs affect the elderly differently than younger people

for many reasons. In old age, the organs function less efficiently. The liver (which metabolizes or breaks down most drugs) and the kidneys (which excrete the breakdown products) reduce the rate at which drugs leave the body. And because there is a higher concentration of fat tissues in an older person, certain drugs can accumulate to higher levels and have more prolonged effects. Studies also indicate that errors are made in administering more than 25 percent of the medication given in nursing homes. This is often a result of inadequate supervision by nurses and physicians, by employment of untrained nurses' aides, and by the lack of adequate government regulation of pharmaceutical suppliers, according to a General Accounting Office report in 1980.

Documenting the negative aspects of health care to the elderly and being aware of what factors lead to greater disability and dependency creates a very depressing picture, but at the same time it provides an impetus for the development of progressively helpful approaches to geriatric care. Already a few medical schools are beginning to approach geriatric concerns in a systematic way, and two new types of doctor are emerging: the geriatric physician and the geriatric psychiatrist. These doctors are trained to be aware of when to use tranquilizers and other psychotropic drugs, and when not to, and which of these medications are the best for elderly patients. They are also trained to listen to their patients' problems and usually have working with them social workers or others trained in treatment and long-term-care planning. Often, they meet with family members and try to work out plans for the patient for obtaining aid such as homemakers or visiting nurses. These doctors look beyond the obvious and do not easily fall into the trap of hasty and incorrect diagnosis of a curable or treatable disease by calling it senility. Unfortunately, it is not easy to locate these specialists, as there are still too few of them. One way to obtain information is to call a major medical complex such as a university-affiliated teaching hospital. If they do not have a geriatric program, they may be able to provide referrals.

Chapter Twelve

The Mythology of Aging

I don't know much about older people, but I would guess that most of them are burdens to their families. Not my mother, though. She has crippling arthritis and can hardly do anything around the house anymore, but I rely on her for advice and companionship. I will miss her if anything happens. . . .

This was said by a woman interviewed in depth about her relationship with her elderly mother, and reflects the ambivalences between private feelings and public attitudes toward aging and older people. On the one hand, we see older people in general terms as demanding, debilitated, disagreeable, and a burden to their families. On the other hand, we consider our own older relatives as people worthy of our affection and assistance.

Perceptions of Old Age

In research studies, respondents have consistently expressed negative attitudes toward the elderly, yet at the same time their actions demonstrate that they are caring and do not dump their elderly kin into old-age homes at the first sign of dependency. According to reports from the National Center for Health Statistics, American families are the primary care-givers, providing the major care for most (80 to 90 percent) of the dependent community-resident elderly who need help. This help may be a trip to the grocery store on a rainy day or it can be total care, depending upon need. Recent research has shown that spouse and children will do their utmost to keep a frail older person at home until the strain becomes too great, and only then will they consider long-term-care facilities. Health problems requiring the giving of injections or the regular use of prescription drugs or the need for frequent visits to the hospital or physician's office, and incontinence, were the main reasons given for seeking admission to nursing homes. However, the decision to institutionalize is often the last resort after heroic efforts to care for older relations fail.

Important in this context is the contrast between *attitudes* toward the elderly and *behaviors* toward relatives. Many attitudinal studies are addressed to feelings about the elderly *in general*, and not to personal feelings for older relatives and friends. This is a crucial distinction which we will explore by comparing the results of older studies with the results of recent investigations.

Since the 1940s, with the publication of a landmark study of attitudes of high school and college students toward supporting aged parents (Dinkel, 1944), research has uncovered a pervasive national sentiment that reinforced the old rocking-chair image of old age as a time of crisis, losses, and isolation; of old people set in their ways, difficult and burdensome.

Old Age as Perceived by Children

Even three- to four-year old children accept the mythic stereotypes of old age, as depicts a (1977) study of 180 children aged three to eleven. These children were of mixed socioeconomic backgrounds from homes in rural communities, the suburbs, and the city. Shown a set of drawings of men of different ages, and asked to give their impressions, they identified the oldest man as "wrinkled," "having no hair and teeth," and "ugly" (Seefeldt, Jantz, Galper, and Serock, 1977). Asked about their preferences in terms of companionship, 58 percent chose the youngest man, while only 13 percent chose the oldest man, with some qualifications. When asked how they imagined they would feel in old age, the majority of the children (108 of

180) said, "I would feel awful," "I'll be nearly dead," "It will be terrible," "I'll be sick and tired and ready to be buried." Only a few (34) said, "I'll be okay," "I'll be rich," "I'll have a house."

In another study, children between five and eight years of age were shown photographs of individuals at different stages of life, from a preschool child to an elderly adult, and asked to rate each subject according to a list of basic characteristics such as ugly, smart, sick, having friends. The superlatives they attributed to the elderly adult were: sickest, meanest, ugliest, loneliest, and so on. When asked to choose the individual they'd be most apt to help and what kind of help they would give, the majority singled out the oldest man and said they would get his glasses, help him shop, push him in a wheelchair, bury him (Weinberger, 1979).

Adolescent Attitudes

Research on attitudes of high school students toward the elderly is limited. Some evidence suggests that adolescents perceive older people as a burden; that in old age (which to them begins at fifty-five) there is no longer any more life satisfaction and nothing to anticipate. Although they perceived their own age group as having the greatest need and capacity for pleasure, they believed that the middle years were the happiest time of life (Ivester and King, 1972).

College Students' Attitudes

More attitudinal studies on aging have been completed with college students than with any other group, largely because psychologists have a captive audience of potential subjects. The majority of these studies also have shown negative attitudes.

In 1978, undergraduates at the University of Maine were given various criteria with which to compare ideal and real older people with ideal and real middle-aged people; consistently, they rated the older adults as more dependent and less effective than the middle-aged people (Sherman and Gold, 1978).

Students at the University of Kansas were asked to comment on summaries of written interviews with two women. In half the summaries, the age of the woman interviewed was said to be thirty-six; in the other half, the age was given as seventy-six years. In both sets of interviews, the women were described as active and had many other similar characteristics.

When the comments were analyzed, it was clear that the students expressed a more positive reaction to the older woman. "She's very active for her age," "She is very young for seventy-six," were typical remarks. However, on other questionnaire items, they showed a bias against older people, which suggests that they may have been favorably impressed by the older woman because her behavior was a striking departure from their expectations (Crockett, Press, and Osterkamp, 1979).

Research literature indicates that ageist attitudes do not soften as people themselves grow older. When people over fifty years have been questioned about their attitudes toward "old people" as a generic group, they, too, viewed them with disaffection and a lack of compassion. However, we are now beginning to see a considerable discrepancy between attitudes and actions.

Do We Really Care?

A high degree of caring and family solidarity was found in a comprehensive study of relationships between spouse or children who are care-givers and the elderly people they support (Teresi, Bennett, and Wilder, 1978). Both the care giver's relatives and the elderly were visited in their homes and interviewed separately so they would not feel constrained by hearing one another's responses. In just over half the cases studied, the spouse was the care-giver. In most other households, the key support person was an adult child, a result very similar to accepted national statistics on the care of aged kin by their families. The age range of care-givers in the survey was nineteen to ninety-four years. The help they provided ranged from very minor assistance with shopping and other chores to total care for the bedridden and housebound.

When these key relatives were questioned about their attitudes toward old people in general, they expressed a definite ageist bias. Relatives of both the dependent and the independent older people showed a similar bias. When the relatives were asked to respond to statements such as, "Most older people are burdens to their families," and "Older people too often make excessive demands of others," a typical response was, "A lot of them drive their kids crazy making demands, but not my husband and me. We stay out of the way, thank God." But the majority were convinced that most older people are burdensome.

Fewer than 5 percent stated, "My parent or spouse is a burden," whereas 41 percent agreed with the statement, "Most older people are a burden to their families."

"My older relative is in good spirits most of the time and is pleasant to have around the house," 85 percent said.

"My older relative doesn't do things to embarrass me or make our friends feel ill at ease when they visit," 87 percent said.

"My older relative does not make excessive demands or interfere with our lives," 85 percent said.

However, when asked the same questions about old people in general, 41 percent agreed that "Most older people make excessive demands," and 86 percent agreed with the general statement that "Most older people get set in their ways and are unable to change." "Not my mother though. She is open to new ideas and is willing to change with the times," 55 percent said. On this point, 45 percent did believe that their elderly relation was set in her ways and unwilling to change (Teresi, Toner, Bennett, and Wilder, 1980).

More Ambivalences

There were strong differences in response about the elderly and decision making in the Teresi et al. (1980) study. Just over half of the care-giver children agreed that older people in general rely on their children to make decisions for them. However, 84 percent said that their elderly parents make their own decisions.

Many respondents (54 percent) were convinced that older people in general prefer to live with younger relatives than live on their own. But 90 percent made statements such as, "My mother would never want to be dependent upon others," and "It's important for Dad to have a sense of independence, which he gets from living on his own."

If we relate to individual older people with affection and respect, why then do we continue to believe in the stereotypes about aging? And has this always been the prevailing attitude? These two questions are deceptively simple and the answers to them are complex.

Historical Views

In primitive societies, fewer people lived to old age, and survival itself was considered an achievement worthy of respect and prestige. The old were honored because it was through them that the customs, geneology, and legends of the tribe were preserved. Location of the best hunting grounds and mastery of primitive skills and medical knowledge were passed from one generation to the next by the elders. The division of labor in a simple society can be closely regulated. Tasks such as hunting and fighting, which require high degrees of strength, stamina, and speed, were carried out by young men. Other tasks, such as settling disputes, offering advice, making essential objects, and telling stories were performed by the older members of the community. With the invention of writing, tribal elders lost one of their important functions, as it was no longer necessary to commit tribal lore to memory. Only in a few primitive societies were the old feared as privileged purveyors of occult information, and only in very poor or nomadic societies, where climate was severe and resources were scarce, were the old and the weak, of necessity, abandoned or left to starve to death. Among tribes that mistreated children, older members were also mistreated. It is interesting to note that in a recent American study, comparing the benefits given to children and elders in state service programs, those states with high levels of public assistance to children tended to provide higher levels of average payments to elders (in Supplementary Security Income [SSI]).

Always Looking for the Fountain of Youth

The ancient world seemed also to hold ambivalent attitudes toward old age. Egyptians recognized the wisdom of older people and rewarded them with status, yet at the same time they avidly sought remedies to reverse the process of aging. One of the first documents written on papyrus, in about 1600 B.C., prescribes a treatment for changing an old man into a young man. It advises eating the fresh glands of young animals.

The Greeks also praised old age while satirizing its weaknesses and eccentricities, as we can see from their literature. Many classic dramas dealt with old age from the point of view of intergenerational conflict.

In the drama *Alcestis*, by Euripides, the Olympian gods have doomed Admetus, the king of Thessaly, to an early death. Apollo then decides to spare him if Admetus can find a substitute who would be willing to die in his place. All those he asks refuse his request, and he bitterly reproaches his parents, who have also refused: He cries out to them, "Old people always say they long for death—their age crushes them—they have lived too long. All words! As soon as death comes near, not a single one wants to go, and age stops being a burden." Admetus finally persuades his devoted wife, Alcestis, to dies in his place, and by the end of the play it is clear that he is not depicted as an admirable character.

In *The Coming of Age*, Simone de Beauvoir traces major events and attitudes affecting the aged from the beginning of recorded history until the time she wrote the book in the early

1960s. By drawing upon countless examples from history, the natural sciences, and the world of art, she analyzes society's attitudes and ambivalences toward the aged. Many critics praised this *catalogue raisonné* as a strong and lucid indictment of society's cruelty and indifference toward older people. Others believed that it contained too much reveling in a mood of bleak pessimism, although even they admit that de Beauvoir has synthesized the cultural and historical attitudes about old age as no other writer has done; also, she has produced a veritable mine of cogent anecdotes for writers to draw upon.

Using ancient Roman history as an example, de Beauvoir traces the close relationship between social stability and high status for the old. The early centuries of the Roman republic were marked by conflict but once private ownership of property was guaranteed by law, a new aristocracy emerged, led by older men who gained privileges and prestige with financial power. For two centuries, while the Senate was ruled by rich property owners who reached high office at a fairly advanced age, the Republic prospered and expanded. But as Rome gained control of Italy by crushing and subjugating its rivals with the force of its military power, the government gradually began to disintegrate and the Senate split into factions. The power and privileges of the old diminished and collapsed, as control "passed into the hands of the soldiers, that is to say of young men," de Beauvoir wrote.

When societies prospered, the elders usually gained in status with their accumulation of wealth and were apt to have low status during periods of civil unrest and rapid change. In Sparta, as in Rome and Venice at their peaks of prosperity, the central governing body was composed of a council of elders. China, with the longest unbroken line in the history of the world, has been a gerontacracy, a nation governed by older people. It would appear that as long as they had the power of the purse, older men were in control.

The status of old people in society should be gauged not only by studying the lives and attitudes toward those in power but also of those who were not in power. Dramatists and historians alike have had a tendency to restrict their observations to the comportment of kings and statesmen and the wealthy, and only occasionally write about the ordinary people, who in early centuries frequently went hungry. The Romans, for instance, established homes for old people, called *gerocomeia*, but very few old people were eligible for them, and old slaves were often left to starve to death.

As Christianity developed, charity was extended to the sick, the destitute, and the disabled as a way to assuage guilt, to increase the likelihood of salvation for the donor, and to promote social cohesion. As early as the fourth century, church-run institutions were being established for people in need in Europe and England, and provision was made for the sick and elderly workers by some, although not very many, feudal lords. By the sixteenth century, many hospitals and almshouses were built, but there were never enough of them to deal with the severe social and health problems of those days.

Until the nineteenth century, only the privileged lived long lives. There were no significant numbers of aged among the poor or middle classes until the Industrial Revolution, at which time the population greatly increased. The rise of technology caused the first big movement away from the farms toward the cities, and along with this rapid change a fervent, religion-based work ethic developed. Its emphasis was on saving, on unremitting hard work, and on the deferral of pleasures. An ambitious middle class began to flourish in a patriarchal era of family-controlled businesses. However, as workers grew old and could not keep up with the ever faster rhythms of change, many died before their time or suffered hardship and poverty if they had no family to take care of them.

The "good old days" when Grandmother cooked and spun and cared for the young, and a hail and hearty white-haired Grandfather repaired farm implements and knew the exact time to sow the wheat and plant the corn, may have been less idyllic than we like to believe. Is it just a continuing myth that past generations had more time and tolerance for the aged? Although religious teaching commanded children to love, honor, and respect their parents, we do not know to what extent such preaching was practiced. We do know that fewer people lived to "see their time out." One day Grandfather was healthy. Suddenly he became ill, the family was called to his bedside, and usually he died before he became a "burden" to his family. There were few hospitals then, no life-support systems, and little knowledge of preventive medicine, so few people lived to frail old age. If they did, families were bigger then, with more children to share the responsibility, and these children usually lived in close proximity to one another and their parents.

Fact and Fiction

Since much knowledge about attitudes toward the elderly comes from the literature written of the time, it is useful to note how contemporary writers treat the old today. According to a study published in 1977, in which researchers analyzed books written between 1950 and 1973 in which older people were either protagonists or played central roles, the prevailing themes were fear of death and loss of self-image. These novels were, in the main, of high literary merit, by such writers as John Updike, Kingsley Amis, Muriel Spark, John Masters, and others who for the most part were well under the age of sixty-five. In general, characterizations of the older protagonists were well developed, but presented an overall picture of passive disengagement, or intergenerational conflict, or Pollyanna-ish unreality. Among the eighty-seven books reviewed, nineteen were about retirement; thirteen were about a power struggle between young and old; eleven dealt with isolation in old age; eight were about the institutionalization of the old; five were concerned with segregated activities in old-age communities; in seven books, the protagonists were portrayed as super human and engaged in activities that would be considered extraordinary for young or old people. A few books mentioned sexual activity, but otherwise there was scant indication to suggest that people in old age can lead normal, active, healthy lives and continue to participate in community activities (Sohngen, 1977).

A survey of recent literature for young children, published in 1977, found an almost total absence of older people. Out of 656 prize-winning children's books, only 41, or 16 percent, contained an older character, and those were either underdeveloped, unexciting, or incidental to the plot (Ansello, 1977).

Television and Ageism

Television is the single most potent medium yet invented for disseminating information, selling products, and creating a basis from which to develop attitudes. Television presents a world of people, places, and situations that attract the attention of average viewers for about thirty hours a week. Heavy viewers spend more time than that at their sets; heavy viewers, according to industry surveys, are young children and retired people. It is curious that these two groups are also the least represented in terms of programming. For over twenty years, social gerontologists have carefully monitored programs and commercials in relation to attitudes toward older people. Findings from the University of Pennsylvania suggest that the more viewers watch television, the more they believe, contrary to fact, that there are fewer old people alive today, and that the majority of them are men. Fewer parts are written for normal middle-aged men and women, and fewer still for older men and women. When older women do appear, they are the character who is most likely to be hurt or killed and to fail. Older men are often portrayed as comic figures, or stubborn and eccentric, and it is most unusual for either sex to be shown having any romantic interests.

"Age on television has been treated as a resource to be distributed as other resources are distributed, along the lines of income, status and power. These patterns are the creation of a system of broadcasting or of story-telling with deep historical, cultural and commercial roots," writes Dr. George Gerbner, director of the Annenburg School of Communication at the University of Pennsylvania.

At the center of virtually every decision made in the television industry are the ratings, which measure the number of viewers, not their appreciation or satisfaction. Ratings determine how much an advertiser will pay for commercial time. The higher the ratings, the more advertisers must pay.

Since the advent of television, the eighteen- to thirty-five-year-old audience has been the prime target for commercials and programming because, according to marketing researchers, buying habits and brand loyalty are established early in life and remain constant. Even though middle-aged people are at the peak of their earning capacity and therefore have more money to spend, advertisers reason that the younger audience is more spendthrift, less demanding as consumers; they exert considerable influence over the family purchases; and have a better recall of commercial messages. More recently, though, television advertisers and producers have become increasingly aware and interested in the growth of the older population and with it, their potential as a viable market. They are beginning to present dramas and talk shows, albeit not yet anywhere near a proportionate number, that consider the special interests of this age group. It is hoped that this indicates a progressive adjustment in attitudes and not just a temporary reaction to fashion and trends.

Age Discrimination in the Work Place

In earlier societies, when change was gradual, the experience and wisdom of the elders represented an important part of learning, and useful work could be found for them to do until the end of their lives. But in a modern industrial society, the rapid development of technology demands constantly changing skills, as well as knowledge and expertise on every level, from labor-intensive farming to the boardroom and assembly line. While people have a longer life span, they seem also to have a shorter work life. Thirty years ago, nearly half of all men sixty-five years and over were in the work force. Today only one in five men of that age and only one woman in twelve hold jobs. In 1982, a report by the House Select Committee on Aging documented a sharp increase in complaints against employers who demoted and discharged workers solely on the basis of their age. This report was based on the growing number of cases filed by workers with the Equal Employment Opportunity Commission (EEOC), and represented a 75 percent increase over the preceding two years. It also stated that the duration of unemployment for older people is about 20 percent longer than the average for the entire population. Under existing law, introduced by Representative Claude D. Pepper, no one between forty and seventy years old can be forced to retire because of age. It is possible that the widespread publicity given to the new age for mandatory retirement made more people aware of their right to complain, but there had to be an increasing number of layoffs as well.

Age Sterotyping and Personnel Decisions

The interactions of age stereotyping on personnel decisions is an area of study for industrial psychologists. In the 1970s, Rosen and Jerdee, industrial psychologists, found that 77 percent of managers questioned thought there should be more affirmative action toward older workers; 60 percent were in favor of eliminating mandatory retirement age altogether. Yet when the same study group was presented with a series of subtle questions requiring considered decisions for the future of marginal employees of varying ages with similar qualifications, 75 percent recommended further training for the younger employees, while only 50 percent recommended the same for older workers.

In another study, Rosen and Jerdee presented executives attending a seminar in personnel management with a work profile of employees aged sixty-two, sixty-five, and sixty-eight, and asked them for their ratings in terms of initiating retirement procedures. The workers under consideration were of equal health and productivity. Each group of executives was given profiles of one age group only. Those who were asked to rate the sixty-eight-year-old workers recommended retirement for them more often than those who rated the younger workers.

Reasons other than confidence in the ability of an older employee will often influence personnel decisions. For instance, older workers holding high-status positions typically command high salaries and represent a large organizational expense. Therefore, some companies consider it more cost-effective to encourage early retirement, replacing older workers with younger ones who receive lower salaries. Other companies believe that it is necessary to project a young image, or that only young whiz kids have up-to-date ideas. The consequences of these attitudes become self-perpetuating.

Societal Attitudes and Social Security

The present cost of retirement is causing grave concern among policymakers, analysts, and the public. Unless major changes are made in the way Americans work and retire, they say, the country could eventually be faced with a serious dilemma: a huge number of retired workers supported by a shrinking base of active wage earners.

Social Security is the main source of income for the majority of retired workers. This fund was set up during the Depression of the 1930s when the aged were among the first to be put out of work and their financial situation became tragic.

At the time, the intentions of President Franklin D. Roosevelt's New Deal administration were twofold: to provide for older Americans and to keep them out of the job market when unemployment was high.

The concept that national governments rather than churches, charities, or families might have to concern themselves with helping the old and the poor is a modern phenomenon. Germany enacted the first pension plan in 1889. It was financed by equal contributions from employers and employees. (United States Social Security is funded the same way.) The scheme was initiated, at a time of rapid industrial expansion and strong agitation for social reform, by then-Chancellor Otto von Bismarck, who is credited with having chosen the sixty-fifth year as a time for retirement, allegedly because he wanted to rid his military high command of some interfering generals who had passed that age marker.

Social Security is America's biggest, most comprehensive, and probably most successful social program. From its inception, benefits have been paid out of taxes deducted from the paychecks of people working that year. These individuals in turn, upon their retirement, will have to rely on benefits from taxes paid by their children's generation. The retirement program set up in 1935 covered workers in commerce and industry only, plus their spouses and dependents. Since then, coverage has been steadily expanded to include farm and domestic workers, the self-employed, members of the armed forces and of religious orders, and others. Retired millionaires collect as well as laborers. Benefits go to almost everyone who has ever paid Social Security taxes and to some people who never have. Housewives who have not worked outside the home and thus never paid into the system collect benefits equal to 50 percent of those earned by their husbands. This plan was based on the social assumption of the time that married women do not work outside their homes, and the system has not been revised to fully accommodate the many women who do. Under the formula for calculating Social Security benefits, married men with wives who have never worked receive the largest return for the dollars they have contributed to the system. A couple consisting of a nonearning wife and a husband whose annual earnings averaged $12,000 a year would receive about 15 percent more in monthly benefits than a couple with the same total income split between a wife and a husband who each earned $6,000 a year.

Critics note that one of the existing flaws in the present Social Security system, which provides monthly benefits to nearly one out of seven Americans, is that it was established on the actuarial assumption of contributions from nine active workers to support each retired worker. Today, that ratio is six to one, and still falling. And there is grave concern about the cost of support to the elderly in thirty to forty years, when the baby-boom generation reaches retirement age. Will the rest of the population be able and willing to support them? Some take the view that the population's willingness to support the elderly will not decline, reasoning that growing old is something that happens to everyone and that there is also deep intergenerational concern. Despite negative attitudes toward old people in general, children and grandchildren do not stand idly by and watch their parents and grandparents live in reduced circumstances, and it seems unlikely that they will in the future. If anything, there is greater awareness of the problems; it is hoped that future generations will have more ingenuity in solving them.

Appendix

A Statistical Overview of the Older Population and Family Support Systems

The Older Population; Now and in the Future

1. According to the 1980 census there are 25.5 million people over age sixty-five residing in the United States; this represents 11.3 percent of the U.S. population. Of this group, about 23.8 million reside in the community. Most of this community-resident group (71 percent) own their homes. A relatively small group (less than 1 percent of the elderly) live in single-room-occupancy hotels; and about 1 percent of the elderly live in congregate housing (housing specially designed for the elderly where at least meals and sometimes other services are provided). (Estimates provided by staff of Department of Housing and Urban Development [HUD].)

2. The 1977 National Center on Health Statistics (NCHS) report on the national nursing home survey indicates that there were 1.3 million individuals residing in skilled nursing facilities and intermediate care facilities. Out of the 1.3 million, 1.1 million were over the age of sixty-five; this group is most likely larger now because most estimates indicate that about 5 percent of the over-sixty-five population resides in nursing homes.

According to a 1980 nationwide survey of board and care homes (funded by Administration on Aging [AOA] to Hebrew Rehabilitation Center for the Aged [HRCA]), there are about 285,000 elderly living in board and care (domiciliary [DCF] care) homes. These figures are rough, so the best estimates of the number of elderly over age sixty-four residing in SNF's, ICF's, and DCF's is between 1.2 and 1.6 million (Teresi, Holmes, and Holmes, 1982).

Breakdown by Age

An important point is that the older population consists of three groups of elderly, with different health problems and service needs. These are the young/old, aged sixty-five to seventy-four; the middle/old, aged seventy-five to eighty-four; and the old/old, aged eighty-five years and over.

1. Currently 61 percent of the older population is between sixty-five and seventy-four years of age; 30 percent are between seventy-five and eighty-four; and 9 percent are eighty-five years of age and over.
2. Examination of the nursing-home population has shown the median age of residents to be eighty-one years. The breakdown by age is: 1.4 percent of the aged sixty-five to seventy-four age group, 6.8 percent of the seventy-five to eighty-four age group, and 21.6 percent of the eighty-five and over group reside in nursing homes.

Some Projections

Examination of the future of the elderly population gives pause for thought.

1. By the year 2000 there will be 32 million individuals aged sixty-five and over in the United States, and it is estimated that in the year 2030, there will be about 55 million elderly (U.S. Senate Special Committee on Aging, 1982). (This will represent 12 percent of the population in the year 2000.)

2. By the year 2030, the overall sixty-five-and-over population will *double*, but the eighty-five-and-over population will *triple*, reaching about 6.6 million individuals (U.S. Bureau of the Census). We know that a large proportion of this group will use institutional and community services, so that the need for and concomitant costs of such services will increase dramatically.

Sex and Marital Status

1. Most elderly individuals in institutional settings are female (71 percent) and most (12 percent) are unmarried; this is compared with 59 percent and 53 percent respectively of the community-resident elderly. However, this is to be expected, because most of the institutional population is over age seventy-four; and we know that among the entire elderly population (institutional and community) aged seventy-five and over, 64 percent are female, and 70 percent of the age group eighty-five and over are female. Only about one fifth of elderly women aged seventy-five and over are married.

2. Among the noninstitutionalized, 48 percent of women aged sixty-five to seventy-four are married compared with 79 percent of men in the same age group. Among the seventy-five-and-over group, only 22 percent of women but 68 percent of men are married. This is in spite of the fact that all but 6 percent of the elderly population sixty-five and over were at one time married. Of the noninstituionalized group age sixty-five and over, almost two thirds of the women and one fourth of the men have no spouse (U.S. Senate Special Committee on Aging Report, 1982).

Dependency

- Only about 4 percent of the noninstitutionalized population are unable to perform one or more self-care activities (dressing, bathing, eating, toileting) compared with 50 to 70 percent of the board and care population and 90 percent of the institutionalized population.

- However, if one considers other types of impairment such as ability to do shopping, cleaning, laundry, and the like, a larger group are impaired (about 8 to 20 percent).
- This means that among the sixty-five-and-over noninstitutionalized population, about 952,000 are dependent in at least one personal self-care activity and as many as 1.9 to 4.8 million elderly may be impaired in instrumental and/or self-care activities.
- Moreover, an analysis by Soldo (1981) of informal supports indicates that of the 8 percent unimpaired in her sample, about 21 percent lacked a spouse or daughter (the primary care giver in most cases). Teresi, Holmes, and Holmes (1982) conclude that this means about 476,000 individuals may be at high risk for institutionalization, and about .95 to 4.8 million elderly may be in need of some form of community-based services or sheltered living arrangement.

Family and Living Arrangement

Most elderly in the community have children with whom they are in frequent contact. For example, Shanas (1979) found that of the four fifths of noninstitutionalized elderly sixty-five and over who have children, about three fourths lived within one half hour of, and had seen at least one of their children within the past week. Family contact among the institutional population is very different. About one half of the nursing home population have no children.

1. About one third (30 percent) of the sixty-five-and-over noninstitutionalized population live alone; about two thirds live with a spouse, child, or other relative. 16 percent of women over age seventy-four live with a child or sibling, and about 15 percent of the sixty-five-to-seventy-four age group have such an arrangement. While only one fifth of women aged fifty-five to sixty-four live alone, about one third of the sixty-five-and-over

group, and about one half of the eighty-five-and-over group live alone.

2. Altogether, about 1.7 million individuals have one or more older parents living in the household (U.S. Senate Special Committee on Aging, 1982).

3. Among the dependent or functionally impaired elderly, the 1977 National Health Interview Survey (NCHS, 1978) indicates that 88 percent reported that relatives provided the major help.

References

American Psychiatric Association, *Diagnostic and Statistical Manual of Mental Disorders*, Third Edition (DSM-III), Washington, D.C., 1979.

Ansello, E.F. "Age and ageism in children's first literature." *Educational Gerontology*, 2:255-274, 1977.

Atchley, R.C. *The Sociology of Retirement*. New York: Halsted Press, 1976.

Blessed, G., B.E. Tomlinson, and M. Roth. "The association betweeen quantitative measures of dementia and of senile change in the cerebral grey matter of elderly subjects." *British Journal of Psychiatry*, 114:797-811, 1968.

Blum, J.E. and Weiner, M.B. "Neurosis in the older adult." In: O.J. Kaplan, (Ed.), *Psychopathology of Aging*. New York: Academic Press, 1979, pp. 167-192.

Butler, R.N. "Looking forward to what?" *American Behavioral Scientist* XIV, Sept. 1970, pp. 121-128.

Butler, R.N. *Why Survive?* New York: Harper & Row, 1975.

———, and Lewis. M.I. *Love and Sex After Sixty*. New York: Harper & Row, 1977.

Crockett, W., Press, A., and Osterkamp. M. "The effect of deviations from stereotyped expectations upon attitudes toward older persons." *Journal of Gerontology*, 34(3):368-374, 1979.

de Beauvoir, Simone, *The Coming of Age*. Editions Gallimard 1970. Translated by Patrick O'Brian, Warner Books, Inc., 1978.

Dinkel, R.M. "Attitudes of children toward supporting aged parent." *American Sociological Review*, 9:370-379, 1944.

Dunlop, B. "Expanded home-based care for the impaired elderly: Solution or pipe dream? *American Journal of Public Health*, 70(5):514-519, 1980.

Essen-Möller, E. "Individual traits of morbidity in a Swedish rural population. *Acta Psychiatr. Neurol. Scand.* (Suppl.), 100:1-161, 1956.

Goldfarb, A.I. "Psychodynamics and the three-generation family." In: E. Shanas and G.F. Streib (Eds.), *Social Structure of the Family: Generational Relations.* Englewood Cliffs, NJ: Prentice-Hall, 1965, pp. 10-45.

Golden, R. A taxometric model for the detection of a conjectured latent taxon. *Multivariate Behavioral Research*, 17:389-416, 1982.

Grad, J. and Sainsbury, P. The effects patients have on their families in a community care and a control psychiatric service—a two-year follow-up. *British Journal of Psychiatry*, 114(3):265-278, 1968.

Gurland, B., Dean L., Cross, P., and Golden, R. The epidemiology of depression and dementia in the elderly: The use of multiple indicators of these conditions. In: J.O. Cole and J.E. Barrett (Eds.), *Psychopathology in the Aged.* New York: Raven Press, 1980, pp. 37-60.

Hebrew Rehabilitation Center for the Aged (HRCA). A nationwide survey of domiciliary care for the aged: Domiciliary care clients and the facilities in which they reside." Authors: S. Sherwood, V. Mor, and C. Gutkin, 1981. Subcontract to Horizon House Institute, "Summary and report of the national survey of state-administered domiciliary care programs in the 50 states and the District of Columbia." Authors: K. Rechstein and L. Bergofsky, 1980.

Hinds, S.W. "The personal and socio-medical aspects of retirement." *Royal Society Health Journal*, 83:281-285, 1963.

Holmes, D. and staff of Community Research Applications. "Differences between residents in intermediate care facilities and residents in domiciliary care facilities." CRA Inc., New York, Dec., 1981.

Ivester, C. and King, K. "Attitudes of adolescents toward the aged." *The Gerontologist*, 17(1):85-89, 1977.

Jarvik, L. and Cohen, D. "A biobehavioral approach to intellectual changes with aging." In: *The Psychology of Adult Development of Aging*, C. Eisdorfer and M.P. Lawton (Eds.). American Psychological Association, Washington, D.C., 1973.

Kahn, R.L., Goldfarb, A.I., Pollack, M., and Peck, A. "Brief objective measures for the determination of mental status in the aged." *American Journal of Psychiatry*, 117(4):326-328, 1960.

Katz, S., Downs, T.D., Cash, H.R., and Grotz, R.C. "Progress in development of the index of ADL." *Gerontologist*, 10:20-30, 1970.

References

Kay, D.W.K. "Epidemiological aspects of organic brain disease in the aged." C.M. Gaitz (Ed.), *Aging and the Brain.* New York: Plenum Press, 1972.

―――, Beamish, P., and Roth, M. "Old age mental disorders in Newcastle-upon-Tyne. I: A study of prevalence." *British Journal of Psychiatry,* 110:146-158, 1964.

Litwak, E., Dono, J., Falbe, C., Kail, B.L., Kulis, S., Marullo, S., Sherman, R. "An empirical and theoretical statement of the differential functions and structures of primary groups amongst the aged. Paper delivered at the Annual American Sociological Society meetings, August 1979.

Mutran, E. and Burke, P. "Feeling useless." *Research on Aging,* 1(2):188-207, 1979.

National Center for Health Statistics. "Current Estimates From the National Health Interview Survey: United States 1977." Hyattsville, Md: Department of Health, Education and Welfare, 1978.

National Center for Health Statistics. "The National Nursing Home Survey, 1977." Hyattsville, Md: U.S. Department of Health, Education, and Welfare, Publication No. 79-1974, 1979.

National Council on Aging. *Fact Book on Aging: A Profile of America's Older Population.* Washington, D.C., February, 1978.

Neugarten, B. *Middle Age and Aging.* Chicago: University of Chicago Press, 1968.

Nunn, C., Bergmann, K., Britton, P.G., Foster, E.M., Hall, E.H., and Kay, D.W.K. "Intelligence and neurosis in old age." *British Journal of Psychiatry,* 124:446-452, 1974.

Pfeiffer, E. "Clinical manifestations of senile dementia." In: K. Nandy (Ed.). *Senile Dementia: A Biomedical Approach.* New York: Elsevier/North-Holland, 1978, pp. 171-184.

Rosen, B., and Jerdee, T.H. "The nature of job-related age stereotypes." *Journal of Applied Psychology.* 61(2):180-183, 1976.

Rosen, B. and Jerdee, T.H. "Too old or not too old." *Harvard Business Review,* 55(6):97-106, 1977.

Rosen, B. and Jerdee, J. H. Influence of employee age, sex, and job status on managerial recommendations for retirement. *Academy of Management Journal,* 22(1):169-173, 1979.

Roth, M. Diagnosis of senile and related forms of dementia. In: R. Katzman, R.D. Terry, and K.L. Bick (Eds.). *Alzheimer's Disease: Senile Dementia and Related Disorders* (Aging, Vol. 7). New York: Raven Press, 1978, pp. 71-85.

―――, "Senile dementia and its borderlands." In: J. Cole and J. Barrett (Eds.). *Psychopathology in the Aged.* New York: Raven Press, 1980, pp. 205-232.

Seefeldt, C., Jantz, R., Galper, A., and Serock, K. "Using pictures to explore children's attitudes toward the elderly." *The Gerontologist*, 17(6):506-509, 1977.

Shanas, E. The Elderly: Family Bureaucracy and Family Help Patterns. Paper presented at Vichy, France, May 1977.

_____, "Social myth and hypothesis: The care of family relatives of old people. *The Gerontologist*, 19:3-9, 1979.

Sherman, N. and Gold, J. "Perceptions of ideal and typical middle and old age." *International Journal of Aging and Human Development*, 1978, pp. 67-73.

Sherwood, S., Greer, D.S., Morris, J.N., and Sherwood, C.C. *The Highland Heights Experiment*. Washington, D.C.: U.S. Government Printing Office, July 1973.

Silverstone, B. and Hyman, H.K. *You and Your Aging Parent*. New York: Pantheon Books, 1976, pp. 202-220.

Sohngen, M. "The experience of old age as depicted in contemporary novels." *The Gerontologist*, 17(1):70-84, 1977.

Soldo, B. Supply of Informal Care Services: Variations and Effects on Service Utilization Patterns. Washington, D.C.: Urban Institute Working Papers, January 1982.

Starr, B. and Weiner, M.B. *The Starr-Weiner Report on Sex and Sexuality in the Mature Years*. New York: Stein & Day, 1981.

Stravinsky, I. *New York Review of Books*, March 14, 1968, p. 8.

Streib, G.F. and Schneider, C.J. *Retirement in American Society: Impact and Process*. New York: Cornell University Press, 1971.

Teresi, J., Bennett, R. and Wilder, D. "Personal time dependency and family attitudes." In: "Proceedings of a Research Utilization Workshop." Community Council of Greater New York, New York, 1978.

Teresi, J., Toner, J., Bennett, R., and Wilder, D. "Discrepancies between attitudes toward older relatives and attitudes toward elderly in general." Paper presented at the 33rd annual meeting of the Gerontological Society, San Diego, CA, November, 1980.

Teresi, J., Holmes, M., and Holmes, D. Sheltered Living Environments for the Elderly. A paper prepared for the Administration on Aging, Office of Human Development Services, August 1982.

Tibbitts, C. "Can we invalidate negative stereotypes of aging?" *The Gerontologist*, 19(1):10-20, 1979.

Torack, R. "Studies in the pathology of dementia." In: C.E. Wells (Ed.). *Dementia*. Philadelphia: F.A. Davis Company, 1971, pp. 111-132.

U.S. Bureau of the Census, Current Population Reports, Series p-25, #704, "Projections of the Population of the United States: 1977 to 2050," 1977.

U.S. Department of Health, Education and Welfare (HEW). Facts About Older Americans. Administration on Aging, Washington, D.C., 1979.

U.S. Department of Health, Education and Welfare. Irelan, L., Motley, D., Schwab, K., Sherman, S., and Murray, J. Almost 65: Baseline Data From the Retirement History Study. Social Security Administration, 1976.

U.S. Senate Special Committee on Aging. *Developments in Aging, 1981*. Vol. I, Special Research 45, March 3, 1981; Washington, D.C., February, 1982.

Weinberger, A. "Stereotyping of the elderly." *Research on Aging*, 1(1):113-136, 1979.

Wurtman, R. Therapeutic Approaches to Dementia. Paper presented at the 33rd annual meeting of the Gerontological Society, San Diego, CA, November, 1980.

Index

A
Activities:
   limitation of, in senile dementia, 40
   loss of interest in, 55
Administration on Aging (AOA), 178
Adolescents' perceptions of old age, 162
Affective disorders, 52-58
Ageism, television and, 170-72
Aging:
   biological aspects of, 134-36
   mythology of, 159-75
   self-image and, 22-23
Agitation, 53
Agnosia, 34-35
Alcestis (Euripides), 166
Alternative living arrangements, 147
Alzheimer's disease, 30, 45, 46
Ambivalence, 75-76, 164-65
American Association of Homes for the Aging, 83
American Health Care Association, 83
American Psychiatric Association, 29
Amis, Kingsley, 170
Angiograms, 43
Ansello, E. F., 170
Anxiety, 53, 54
Apraxia, 34-35
Atchley, R. C., 111
Awareness of pain, 23-24

B
Balance mechanisms, 135
Beauvoir, Simone de, 166-67
Behavior, parents as regulators of, 12-14
Behavioral problems, 49-65
   assessing risks of, 64-65
   cognitive, 59-60

Bennett, R., 163, 164
Biological aspects of aging, 134-36
Bismarck, Otto von, 174
Blessed, G., 38
Blum, J. E., 58
Bowel and bladder control, loss of, 41
Britain, 149-50
Browning, Robert, 131
Bureaucracy, 148-50
Burke, P., 138
Butler, Robert N., 25, 45, 117, 126-27, 129, 133, 155

C
Cardiovascular diseases, 45
CAT scans (computerized axial tomography), 43
Census Bureau, U.S., 180
Children's perceptions of old age, 161-62
China, 168
Choline, 46-47
Chronic dementias, 30-31
Cognitive disorders, 59-60
   in senile dementia, 38-39
Cohen, D., 136
College students' perceptions of old age, 162-63
Coming of Age, The (Beauvoir), 166-67
Complaining:
   chronic, 105
   as form of communication, 91-92
Concentration, lack of, 56
Concreteness, 63
Confabulation, 63-64
Congress, U.S., 110
Continence, 41
Cornell University, 112
Cowley, Malcolm, 103
Crockett, W., 163

187

D

Daughter, overly dutiful, 16-19
Demoralization, 56
Dependency, 4-5
   of frail elderly, 144-46
   of wives, 20-22
Depression, 52-57
   help for, 55-57
   masked, 104-5
Diagnostic and Statistical Manual of Mental Disorders (DSM-III), 29, 55
Diagnostic techniques:
   medical, 42-43
   psychiatric, 41-42
Dinkel, R. M., 161
Domiciliary care facilities (DCFs), 84
Doom, feelings of, 56
Drachman, 47
Dressing, limitations on, 40
Drugs, 155-56
   intoxication from, 44
   reactions to, 46
Dunlop, B., 150

E

Eating, limitations on, 40
Ego, 13
   See also Family ego
Egypt, ancient, 166
Electroencephalograms (EEGs), 43
Emotional responses, 8-9
Energy loss, 55
Equal Employment Opportunity Commission (EEOC), 172
Essen-Moller, E., 32
Euripides, 166
Extended family, 137

F

Family:
   changes in, 6-8, 98-99
   coping strategies for, 90-91
   critical periods in, 97-107
   extended, 137
   fear of separation and, 121-22
   future, 9-10
   as link between patient and staff, 89-90
   nursing home placement and, 77-95
   as primary care giver, 5-6, 147-48, 150
   stages of, 120-21
   surviving death in, 122-23
   in treatment of senile dementia, 47-48
Family ego:
   adaptation to change and, 11-24
   aging and self-image in, 22-23
   awareness of pain in, 23-24
   dependent wife in, 20-22
   divided, 14-16
   overly dutiful daughter in, 16-19
   reversing past in, 19-20
Feeding, parents as regulators of, 12-14
Feelings, understanding one's own, 71-72

Frail elderly, 143-57
   alternative living arrangements for, 147
   bureaucracy and, 148-50
   coping with emergencies, 146-47
   dependency of, 144-46
   family as primary care giver for, 147-48, 150
   medical attitudes toward, 154-57
   in nursing homes, 151-53
Frank, Jerome, 54
Freud, Sigmund, 13

G

General Accounting Office, 156
Gerbner, George, 171
Gold, J., 162
Golden, R., 32
Goldfarb, Alvin, 41, 145
Grad, 149
Gray Panthers, 139
Greece, ancient, 166
Growing Young (Montague), 77
Guilt, nursing home placement and, 81-82
Gurland, B., 32

H

Hate and love, 75-76
Health, retirement and, 111-12
Health, Education and Welfare, U.S. Department of, 114
Hebrew Rehabilitation Center for the Aged (HRCA), 178
Helplessness, 54
Highland Heights project, 147
Hinds, S. W., 111
Holmes, D., 84, 187
Holmes, M., 187
Holmes, Oliver Wendell, Sr., 109
Hopelessness, 54
Hoshi, Saigyo, 49
House Select Committee on Aging, 172
Household tasks, limitations on, 40
Housing and Urban Development, U.S. Department of, 178
Hyman, H. K., 88
Hypochondriasis, 59, 104-5

I

Id, 13
Impulses, primitive, 62-64
Individual basic needs, 8-9
Infections, 45
Intelligence, 136
Intermediate care facilities (ICFs), 84
   relocation to, 93
International Herald-Tribune, 151-52
Ivester, C., 162

J

Jakob-Creutzfeldt's disease, 30
Jarvik, L., 136
Jerdee, 173
Johnson, Samuel, 67

K

Kahn, Robert, 41
Kansas, University of, 163

Kay, D. W. K., 32
Kierkegaard, Søren, 119
Kuhn, Maggie, 139
Kunitz, Stanley, 143

L
Lennon, John, 1
Lewis, M. I., 129, 155
Life of Johnson (Boswell), 67
Litwak, Eugene, 150
Longevity, 2-3
Love and hate, 75-76

M
McCartney, Paul, 1
Maine, University of, 162
Masked depression, 104-5
Massachusetts Institute of Technology (MIT), 46, 47
Masters, John, 170
Medical diagnostic techniques, 42-43
Mental Status Questionnaire (MSQ), 41-42
Metabolic problems, 46
Minnesota Multiphasic Personality Inventory (MMPI), 42
Montague, Ashley, 77
Mother-daughter interaction, 99-102
Mourning, 122-24
Mutran, E., 138
Mythologies of aging, 159-75

N
National Center for Health Statistics, 160, 178
National Institute of Health, 133
Needs:
  basic, 8-9
  symptoms of, 106-7
Nervousness, 54
Nonreinforcement, 70
Northwestern University, 47
Nunn, C., 44
Nursing home placement, 77-95
  burden of guilt in, 81-82
  cooperation and compromise in, 79-81
  family roles in, 78-79
  finding suitable facility, 83
  including elderly in decisions, 82
  levels of care and, 83-85
  neglect in, 151-53
  transition from home to, 88-89
  visits and, 92

O
Office of Research and Statistics, Social Security Administration, 114
One-sided conversations, 70-71
Osterkamp, M., 163
Overly dutiful daughter, 16-19

P
Pain, awareness of, 23-24
Paranoid disorders, 60-61
Parents:
  death of, 124
  as regulators of feeding and behavior, 12-14

Pennsylvania, University of, 171
Pepper, Claude D., 172
Perceptions of old age, 160-63
Perseveration, 34
Personality changes in senile dementia, 39-40
PET scans (positron emission tomography), 43
Pfeiffer, Eric, 29, 33
Pick's disease, 30, 45
Press, A., 163
Primitive societies, 165-66
Proust, Marcel, 124
Pseudodementias, 45-46
Psychiatric diagnostic techniques, 41-42
Psychoses and primitive impulses, 62-64

R
Reality orientation, 74
Reality testing, loss of, 60
Relocation, stress of, 93-94
Retirement, 109-18
  case study of, 116-17
  health and well-being and, 111-12
  as new phenomenon, 110-11
  research findings on, 114-16
  right to work and, 117-18
  self-esteem and, 112-14
Right to work, 117-18
Rome, ancient, 167-68
Roosevelt, Franklin D., 174
Rosen, 173
Roth, Martin, 31-32, 41, 44, 184

S
Sadness, 54
Sainsbury, 149
Schizophrenia, 61
Schneider, C. J., 112
SDAT, *see* Alzheimer's disease
Self-blame, 55
Self-esteem, retirement and, 112-14
Self-image, aging and, 22-23
Seefeldt, C., 161
Senate Special Committee on Aging, 179, 180, 182
Senile dementia, 25-48
  activity limitation in, 40
  agnosia and apraxia in, 34-35
  causes of, 31-32
  chronic, 30-31
  classic core symptoms of, 29
  clinical assessment of cognitive functioning in, 38-39
  clinical assessment of personality changes in, 39-40
  continence in, 41
  early stages of, 27-28
  final stages of, 28-29
  hiding signs of, 35-37
  incidence rates of, 32-33
  individual reactions to onset of, 33-34
  medical diagnostic techniques in, 42-43
  mistaken diagnosis of, 43-46
  perseveration in, 34
  psychiatric diagnostic techniques in, 41-42

Senile dementia (*cont.*)
    sudden onset, 29-30
    treatment for, 46-48
Separation, fear of, 121-22
Sexuality, 128-30, 134-35
Shanas, Ethel, 11
Sherman, N., 162
Sherwood, S., 147
Silverstone, B., 88
Skilled nursing facilities (SNFs), 84-86
Skull X-rays, 43
Sleep difficulty, severe, 55
Social Security, 174-75
Social Secueity Act (1935), 110
Social Security Administration, 114
Sociology of Retirement, The (Atchley), 111
Sohngen, M., 170
Soldo, B., 181
Somatic complaints and disorders, 54, 59
Spark, Muriel, 170
Sparta, 168
Starr, B., 129, 135
Streib, G. F., 112
Stress of relocation, 93-94
Sudden onset dementia, 29-30
Suicidal thoughts, 57-58
    depression and, 55
Superego, 13
Symptoms of needs, 106-7

T
Television, ageism and, 170-72
Teresi, J., 163, 164, 179
Tibbitts, C., 118
Tomlinson, B. E., 184
Toner, 164

Toxin ingestions, 46
Tumors, 45

U
Updike, John, 169-70

V
Venice, 168
Vitamin deficiencies, 45
Visits, nursing home, 92

W
Wechsler Adult Intelligence Scale (WAIS), 42, 136
Weight change, 55
Weinberger, A., 162
Weiner, M. B., 58, 129, 135
Well-being, retirement and, 111-12
Why Survive? Being Old in America (Butler), 45, 117
Widows and widowers:
    adaptation to living alone by, 124-28
    mourning by, 123-24
Wilder, 163, 164
Wish to die, *see* Suicidal thoughts
Wives, dependent, 20-22
Women, sexuality of, 129-30
Work place, age discrimination in, 172-73
Wurtman, Dr., 47

Y
You and Your Aging Parent (Silverstone and Hyman), 88
"Young/old" people, 131-41
    diversity of, 132-33
    new breed of, 138-41